Editor
Mary Kaye Taggart

Editorial Manager
Karen J. Goldfluss, M.S. Ed.

Editor-in-Chief
Sharon Coan, M.S. Ed.

Illustrator
Bruce Hedges

Interior Art Design
Michelle M. McAuliffe
Marsha W. Black

Cover Artist
Denise Bauer

Art Coordinator
Cheri Macoubrie Wilson

Creative Director
Elayne Roberts

Product Manager
Phil Garcia

Imaging
James Edward Grace

Publisher
Mary D. Smith, M.S. Ed.

BUSY TEACHER'S GUIDE
ART LESSONS

Grades 1-3

Authors

Michelle M. McAuliffe
Marsha W. Black

Teacher Created Resources, Inc.
6421 Industry Way
Westminster, CA 92683
www.teachercreated.com

ISBN: 978-1-57690-210-3

©1999 Teacher Created Resources, Inc.
Reprinted, 2009
Made in U.S.A.

Table of Contents

Table of Contents *(cont.)*

Introduction

Elementary art education exists as an important developmental tool for the nurturing of creative and academic skills in young children. It helps in the process of sharpening the senses and aids in developing hand-eye coordination. It contributes significantly to small muscle control. Art assists in maturing the mind and emotions of the child through its educational and formative qualities.

The importance of art as an element in educational curricula cannot be overstated. Children have a basic need to express themselves by making things. Color and form offer the child opportunities for creative responses to awaken dormant images within the imagination and assist in bringing these images into tangible reality.

Ideas must be converted by the child into visual language, with the teacher acting as a guide in an accepting environment. The teacher can accomplish this through suggestion and encouragement while allowing the child to work freely and without undue interference. This will give the child a sense of accomplishment and joy.

Art is a civilizing and cultural influence. Children should be taught to appreciate art during their formative years. The authors created this book to help teachers nurture and bring to fruition each child's creative talents.

How to Use This Book

Busy Teacher's Guide: Art Lessons is designed to make the teaching of art an easy and enjoyable experience for all teachers. The projects in this book have been tested thoroughly, first by the authors and then in the classroom. The testing should reassure the instructor that the finished projects will be functional and attractive.

The teacher who selects this book as an art text will have more than enough projects for the entire school year. Students will learn the basic elements of art and how to apply them. Some lessons are designed to help sharpen their drawing skills, while others will introduce a variety of techniques and materials. Also, holiday projects are included which the teacher can use to decorate the classroom or send home with the students are included.

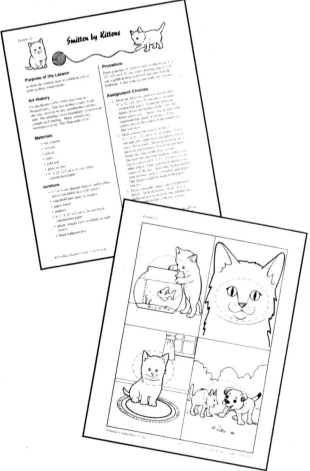

Many states now have proficiency standards for art; the lessons in this book will meet many of these requirements. Teachers will find it easy to choose specific skills to strengthen their students' weak points. The lessons can be simplified or made more complex depending on the backgrounds of the students involved.

When students apply a variety of techniques and work with many different materials they increase their competency in the theory and practice of art. The students will also add new terms (which are informally introduced in the lessons) to their art vocabularies.

Introduction *(cont.)*

How to Use This Book *(cont.)*

This book is designed to meet the needs of busy teachers. Each lesson has a "Purpose" ready to be copied into a lesson plan book. Each lesson also has an "Art History" section which describes a famous artist and his or her artwork. It would be beneficial to show these famous artworks to the students and discuss them. (Some sources for the art are listed on page 80.) The materials needed for each student to complete the main project are listed in the "Materials" section. Any additional materials needed to complete the "Assignment Choices" are listed under the subheading "Variations." The listed materials are readily available and reasonably priced. Many may be recycled from everyday items. (**Note to the teacher:** Some of the lessons list soy crayons in the "Materials" section. They are nontoxic, brighter in color that other crayons, non-flaking, and easily blended. They may be purchased under the trade name Prang Fun Pro. For more information, contact their Web page at *http://www.dixonticonderoga.com* or their consumer line at 1-800-824-9430.) The "Procedure" section of each lesson is written to the teacher and gives directions for the main art project. The "Assignment Choices" section is student-directed and it gives the students one or more variations on the main project from which to choose. The "Connection" section points out a link between the artist highlighted in the "Art History" section and the lesson. Finally, on the page opposite each lesson, patterns for and/or illustrations of the finished work are provided to help the teacher visualize the completed work. In addition to prepared lessons, you will find a generic form on pages 78 and 79 which may be used to create your own lessons.

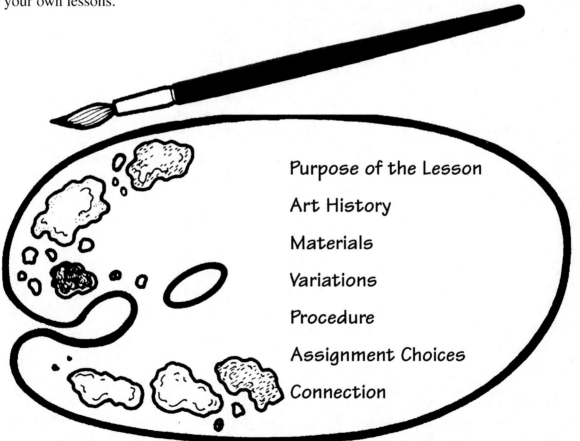

Purpose of the Lesson

Art History

Materials

Variations

Procedure

Assignment Choices

Connection

Gentle, constructive criticism of finished or in-progress work will help the growth of an elementary student's skill level. Criticism, however, should always be accompanied by compliments about what is good in the individual student's work. A pupil's enthusiasm and hard work are the mark of a competent teacher.

Color Magic

Purpose of the Lesson

to explain that the primary colors (red, yellow, and blue) cannot be produced by mixing, but the secondary colors (orange, green, and violet) can be produced by mixing certain primary colors together

Art History

Franz Marc (1880–1916), a native of Germany, received much of his inspiration from French painters who loved bright colors. He did not paint things as you would see them in nature. For example, he painted horses blue with bright backgrounds of sometimes clashing colors. His painting "Grazing Horses" shows his great love for color mixing.

Materials

- watercolor or tempera paints
- glue or paste
- scissors
- crayons or markers
- pencil
- brushes
- construction paper scraps

Procedure

Draw four hot air balloons. Overlap them as shown in the picture or duplicate the next page. Paint the first balloon blue and the second one yellow. The overlapping section will turn green. Paint the third balloon red, and the overlapping section will become orange. Paint the last section blue. The overlapping section will become purple.

Outline the balloons with a black crayon or marker. Add details to the teddy bears, baskets, and scenery by using construction paper scraps and/or markers.

Assignment Choices

1. Draw overlapping vases and jars in interesting shapes and sizes. Overlap the primary colors to create the secondary colors.

2. Make a scribble design to create overlapping forms. Color in the created forms with crayons or paints. Overlap the primary colors to make the secondary colors. Add texture and use markers to add accents.

3. Draw a textured basket and then fill it with overlapping flowers of many varieties. Overlap the primary colors to create the secondary colors.

4. Create a wallpaper design with long, wavy lines that overlap. Use primary and secondary colors to complete your wallpaper pattern.

Connection

Franz Marc used color in unusual ways. His paintings reveal masterfully mixed colors, and he invented many new ways to use shades and hues.

Like Franz Marc, the students should also be adventurous in their use of color. It is not always necessary to be faithful to the colors in nature. However, the teacher should be sure that the students understand the difference between primary and secondary colors and that they know how to mix them.

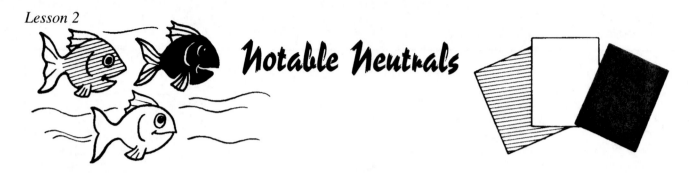

Notable Neutrals

Purpose of the Lesson

to explain to the students the function of neutrals in relation to the color spectrum

Art History

Kay Sage (1898–1963) was born in New York. Critics have described her as a brilliant artist. She was a surrealist painter who painted real objects in mysterious ways. Her painting "I Saw Three Cities" was painted in colors that were so subtle that they seemed to be neutrals.

Note: Neutrals (white, black, and gray) do not have any color. They allow artists to tone colors by mixing tints and shades. They are always compatible with any color because they do not reflect any wavelength of light in the spectrum. This principle might be helpful to students when they select paper for mounting their works of art.

Materials

- 8 ½" x 11" (22 cm x 28 cm) white construction paper
- pencil
- fine-point black marker
- gray chalk
- scissors
- paste
- red construction paper
- superhold hair spray

Variations

- newspapers (want ads)
- scrap paper
- 8 ½" x 11" (22 cm x 28 cm) sea green construction paper

Procedure

On a piece of white paper, make a pencil sketch of a jungle animal, dinosaur, or other creature of your choice. Carefully trace the pencil lines with a fine-point black marker. Shade some areas with gray chalk. Spray your finished picture with a thin coating of superhold hair spray. Cut out the creature around the edges and mount it on red construction paper.

Assignment Choices

1. Choose a musical instrument or some other kind of noisemaker. Sketch it on a piece of scrap paper. Cut out the pattern and trace it onto newsprint. Paste the newsprint cutouts onto white construction paper. Add details to the instrument or noisemaker with a black marker.

2. Use your imagination to make an interesting seascape. Sketch the main elements of your seascape on a piece of white paper. Cut out these patterns and trace them onto newsprint. Cut out the newsprint shapes and paste them onto a piece of sea green construction paper. Add details with a black marker.

3. Use a pencil to sketch a composition on a piece of white construction paper. Draw a mouse and cheese or think of your own subject matter. Trace your sketch with gray and black markers.

Connection

Students will learn from this lesson that neutrals are helpful to all artists. They may be mixed with spectrum colors to lighten or darken them into myriad tints and shades. Neutrals are also always compatible with any color or combination of colors. Kay Sage made masterful paintings by using neutrals with just a hint of color.

The Shape of Things

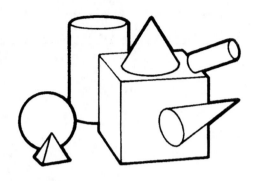

Purpose of the Lesson

to show the students that many tangible things consist of a variety of basic shapes

Art History

Romare Bearden (1911–1988) was born in North Carolina. He was best known for his collages in which he used shapes cut from paper and other materials. His charming picture "The Morning of the Rooster" has a variety of basic shapes. In this composition, Romare Bearden captured the peaceful interior of a home in a small southern community.

Materials

- construction paper
- glue or paste
- crayons
- pencil
- ruler
- scissors
- variety of magazine pictures (for teacher's demonstration)

Variations

- textured-looking materials cut from magazines

Procedure

Teacher: Draw a triangle, circle, square, rectangle, cone, and cylinder on the chalkboard. Show students that many things are combinations of basic shapes. Point out some of these basic shapes in magazine pictures. Help them find basic shapes in other things in their own environment.

Show the students how shapes can be shaded to look three-dimensional. Then demonstrate how basic shapes can be combined to make concrete and abstract designs.

Student: Complete the teddy bear on the next page by cutting out shapes from construction paper and gluing them onto the picture. You may wish to create your own teddy bear out of construction paper shapes on a separate piece of paper. Add details of your own so that your bear has its own personality. It may be helpful to study each part of the bear to understand the underlying shapes in the drawing.

Assignment Choices

1. Choose an animal and draw it. Search for the basic shapes within your drawing and label them.
2. Draw, cut out, and arrange a triangle, circle, square, rectangle, cone, and cylinder to create an abstract design. Glue the shapes in place.
3. Draw some basic shapes. Shade them in order to give them a three-dimensional appearance.
4. Use three basic shapes and textured materials to make a composition. The three shapes may be used as many times as you need for your composition. Try overlapping the shapes. Explore a variety of combinations before pasting them onto a background.

Connection

Romare Bearden saw art everywhere, even in discarded materials. This lesson will help students analyze and simplify complex pictures. It will also build up their confidence in their drawing abilities when they realize that all pictures are a combination of basic shapes.

Line Design

Purpose of the Lesson

to help the students understand why lines are important in drawing, design, and painting

Art History

Ben Shahn (1898–1969), an American artist, used lines in his artwork to communicate his feelings about social issues such as labor movements, race relations, and welfare. Ben Shahn's composition "Still Music" is an example of his effective use of lines.

Materials

- colored chalk
- pencil
- fine-tip black marker
- 9" x 12" (23 cm x 31 cm) white drawing paper
- old magazines
- music
- fixative or superhold hair spray

Variations

- fine-tip markers of various colors
- colored pencils
- 12" x 18" (31 cm x 46 cm) white drawing paper
- wallpaper books
- copies of *National Geographic*
- seed catalogs
- copies of *Ranger Rick* magazine
- light shades of 9" x 12" (23 cm x 31 cm) construction paper

Procedure

Teacher: Before beginning this lesson, explain that lines can powerfully convey feelings of happiness, sadness, fear, courage, beauty, and anger. They may be curved, short, thin, wavy, broken, jagged, thick, uneven, rhythmical, perpendicular, vertical, or horizontal. Motion is

created using lines, much like skaters on ice. Lines should sing. When drawing, do not make cramped, shaky lines. Instead, they should be smooth and drawn quickly. Practice will improve the quality of lines.

Help inspire students in choosing the subject for their artwork by playing classical and contemporary music. Also, allow them to look through magazines for ideas.

Student: Use several brightly-colored pieces of chalk to create a background on white paper. Fill the entire page with sections of color. Spray (with your teacher's help) the background with a fixative or super-hold hair spray. Pencil in lines on the background to create movement and rhythm. Go over the pencil lines with a fine-tip, black marker. Make the lines interesting by using various widths.

Assignment Choices

1. Look at pictures of animals in magazines such as *National Geographic* or *Ranger Rick*. Draw a picture of an animal of your choice or draw the face of another student in your class. Try to show expressions on the face in your picture. Trace over your lines with colored markers.
2. Look for seed catalogs or expired wallpaper books for ideas of floral or plant designs. Draw a picture of the plants or flowers on a piece of pastel construction paper. Add stems and leaves to fill the page. Outline your drawing with bright markers.
3. Create a line design of your choice on pastel construction paper. Use pencils or markers.

Connection

Ben Shahn used lines to effectively emphasize the colors and shapes of his pictures. Do the lines in your art "sing"? What stories do the lines tell?

Veggie Values

Purpose of the Lesson

to explain to the students how to give an object (or a region) depth by shading in light and dark areas and to teach about the nuances of shading, which are known as *values*

Art History

Georges Braque (1882–1963) was born in France. He, along with his colleague Pablo Picasso, invented cubism (the rendering of an object from multiple viewpoints). His painting "Le Jour" ("The Day") is a good example of Braque's use of value in a composition.

Materials

- white construction paper 12" x 18" (31 cm x 46 cm)
- old seed catalogs
- scissors
- glue
- brown paper sacks
- tissues
- paper towels
- superhold hair spray or fixative
- pencil
- bright colors of chalk

Variations

- soy crayons
- women's magazines
- corrugated box material
- raffia or paper ribbon

Procedure

Teacher: Cut out pictures of vegetables from seed catalogs and display them. Point out to students that the shading on the vegetables looks darker along the edges and lighter near their middles. This makes the vegetables seem to have thickness and depth. As students begin this project, show them how to do similar shading with chalk.

Student: Cut out a basket shape from a brown paper sack. Cut a slit across the top of the basket as shown on the opposite page. (You may use a bowl or other shape, if you would prefer.)

Choose some colorful vegetables from the opposite page and draw as many as you need to fill the basket. Shade the vegetables and color them with bright chalk. Spray them (with your teacher's help) with superhold hair spray. Cut out the vegetables and arrange them in the basket. Glue them in place and add an interesting background with chalk. Finally, spray the finished project.

Assignment Choices

1. Cut a strip of paper 12" x 1" (31 cm x 3 cm). You may trace around the edges of a one-foot ruler to do this. Draw a centered line going down the length of the strip and then lay it aside. Make a pattern in the shape of a pepper (see the next page). Use the pattern to draw some peppers on a piece of white paper. Color them with red, yellow, and green soy crayons. Cut out the peppers and paste them to the center of the paper strip. Add a paper fastener to the top to hang your arrangement.

Connection

In this lesson, the students should learn to give their drawings the appearance of having a third dimension. When working on a two-dimensional place, shading "fools the eye" into perceiving a third dimension to that object. Students should apply color and shading values to projects where thickness is desired, just as Georges Braque did.

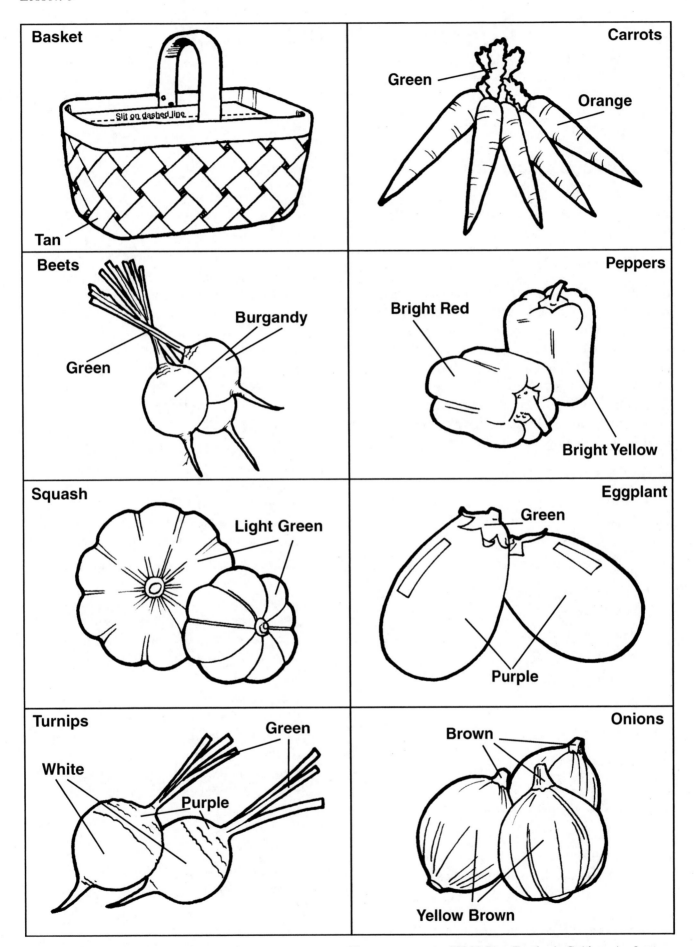

Basket

Tan

Carrots

Green

Orange

Beets

Burgandy

Green

Peppers

Bright Red

Bright Yellow

Squash

Light Green

Eggplant

Green

Purple

Turnips

Green

White

Purple

Onions

Brown

Yellow Brown

Itty-Bitty Animal Infants

Purpose of the Lesson

to give the students experience in working with a variety of textures and practice in using circles as the basis for drawings

Art History

Lavinia Fontana (1552–1614), a native of Italy, was a wealthy and famous artist at a time when women were rarely recognized as having artistic talent. She used texture so well in her paintings that viewers often felt as if they could reach out and touch the subject matter. She was the official painter for the papal court and a mother of eleven children. Her painting "Portrait of a Lady with a Lapdog" is a masterpiece.

Materials

- furry fabric
- dried grass
- glue
- pencil
- plastic wiggly eyes (available in craft and fabric stores)
- white paper
- pink felt
- clear, nylon fishing line
- scissors

Variations

- tree bark
- crayons
- feathers (available in craft stores)
- twigs
- English walnut shells
- almond-shaped, green glass eyes (available in craft stores)
- craft sticks

Procedure

Teacher: Dried grass and small weeds may be gathered and pressed in the pages of a book a few days prior to starting this project.

Student: Draw two or more circles to create the basic form of a rabbit and then draw the rabbit. Cover your drawing with furry fabric. Paste on pink felt for the ears and nose. Add a pair of wiggly eyes and lengths of fishing line for whiskers. Make an environment of dried grasses for your rabbit.

Assignment Choices

1. Using circles as the basis of your drawing, draw a squirrel on a tree limb. Paste bark pieces on the tree. Cover the squirrel with fuzzy, brown fabric. Add some plastic, wiggly eyes and color the nose with a black marker. Split several walnut shells in half and glue them at the squirrel's feet.

2. Using circles as the basis of your drawing, draw a nest with young birds in it. Show it in a tree with foliage. Paste twigs and grass on the nest and bark on the tree. Cut some feathers to the needed size and paste them on the birds. Give your birds eyes.

3. At the bottom of a piece of paper, paste craft sticks to make a fence configuration. Color the fence with crayons. Using circles as the basis of your drawing, draw a cat on the fence. Cover the cat with furry fabric. Paste on pink felt for a nose and add green glass eyes. Make whiskers out of fishing line and carefully glue them on.

Connection

In this lesson the students will have the experience of working with many textures.

The Case for Space

Purpose of the Lesson

to show how to use certain elements of art to create an ordered and balanced picture plane that is pleasing to the eye

Art History

René Magritte (1898–1967) was born in Belgium. A surrealist painter and skillful technician, Magritte used space in a creative way which gave new contexts to ordinary objects. His painting "The Voice of Space" is an example of what critics termed "magic realism" because of his masterful talent in creating spatial relationships.

Materials

- two lightweight, plastic-coated hangers
- yarn to match the hangers
- #30 test, monofilament fishing line
- white tagboard
- pencil
- colored markers
- scissors

Variations

- 9" x 12" (23 cm x 31 cm) white drawing paper
- old magazines
- paste
- ruler
- thick and thin markers
- ballpoint pen
- scrap paper

Procedure

Teacher: You might want to begin this lesson by letting the students study some of Alexander Calder's mobiles. This will help them as they construct their own mobiles (see below). You might need to help them with the first step of twisting the two hangers together for the frame of the mobile. This project will show the students that space outside of the picture plane may also be changed.

For the "Assignment Choices" projects, emphasize to the students the challenge of a blank piece of paper. Ask them to think of the infinite number of possibilities for breaking up space on a picture plane.

Student: Grasp one hanger at a time by the middle and bend the bottom wire up to the hook. After doing this to both hangers, position the arms perpendicular to each other as shown in the diagram on the next page. Tie the two hangers together firmly in this position with two or three strands of yarn. Twist and bend the hooks together and cover them with yarn. Attach fishing line to the four arms of the hangers and one piece to the middle. On tagboard, draw forms from space (stars, comets, sun, moon, planets, etc.). Cut out the forms and brightly color both sides. Attach them to the fishing line.

Assignment Choices

1. Draw three-dimensional forms and integrate them into one composition. Accent your work with markers or crayons.

2. Draw a line form to fill a piece of white drawing paper. Fill its spaces with texture created by pen lines or clipped from magazines and cut to shape. (Paste the magazine shapes in place if you are using this technique.) Using nontextured material between textured pieces will enhance the composition.

Connection

In this lesson, students will learn techniques of using negative space to accentuate the forms chosen for positive space, as René Magritte did. This technique is basic to all artwork, and should be stressed repeatedly.

Changing space outside the picture plane

Changing space with solids

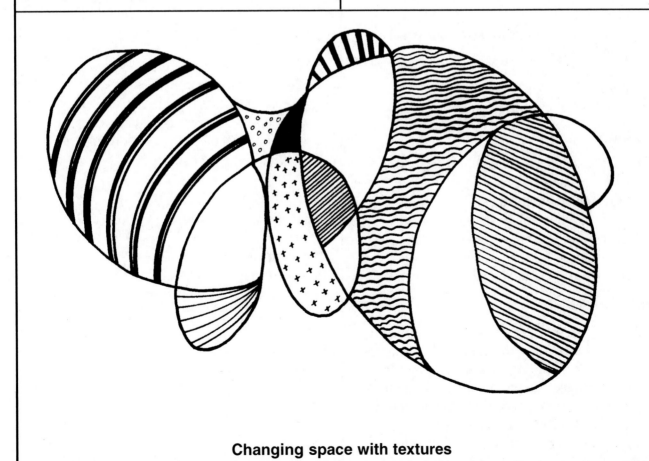

Changing space with textures

Meltdown Marvels

Purpose of the Lesson

to explore a variety of melted crayon textures, and to be aware of the total appearance of the art, which is known as form

Art History

Vincent van Gogh (1853–1890) was a native of the Netherlands. Many of his paintings are of vases with flowers. His technique in "Roses and Anemones" is one of heavy impasto, which he used to create an interesting texture.

Materials

- 9" x 12" (23 cm x 31 cm) white construction paper
- pencil
- clear glue
- broken pieces of crayon (remove paper)
- paintbrushes
- electric warming tray
- muffin pan or metal jar lids
- metallic crayons or glitter

Variations

- crayon shavings, divided into egg carton compartments by color.
- gray construction paper
- black acrylic paint or marker
- heavy cardboard
- electric iron for the teacher
- light blue construction paper

Procedure

Teacher: This art activity is an excellent way to recycle broken crayons. Sort the broken crayons by color, place them into the cups of a muffin pan, and place the pan on top of a warming tray for melting. Extra supervision (adult volunteers) will be needed. Divide the students into manageable groups. Only one group of children should work with melted crayons at a time. Groups who are waiting for their turns should be given alternative projects which need no supervision.

Student: On a piece of white construction paper, make a 1" (2.54 cm) border around the perimeter. Draw a flower arrangement and vase within the border, or you may simply use a copy of the following page. Use paintbrushes to apply the melted crayons to your picture. Accent your work with metallic crayons or sprinkle glitter over clear glue.

Assignment Choices

1. Sketch a picture on gray construction paper. Use a paintbrush to apply melted crayons. Make accents by using a paintbrush and black acrylic paint or a fine-tip black marker.

2. Glue heavy cardboard under a piece of light blue construction paper. Draw a landscape. Use paintbrushes to build up layers of melted crayon wax on the trees, mountains, etc. This will give them a three-dimensional effect.

Connection

Vincent van Gogh used thick paints to create texture and to give his flowers a lifelike quality. The students will learn the value of texture in their art through this lesson.

Perspective Objective

Purpose of the Lesson

to introduce the concept of simple perspective to the students

Art History

Charles Demuth (1883–1935) was born in Pennsylvania. He is well known for his still lifes and flower arrangements. His picture "Figure Five in Gold" helps the viewer travel in depth into the picture by showing the same object smaller and smaller within the picture's plane.

Materials

- 12" x 18" (31 cm x 46 cm) white drawing paper
- pencil
- soy crayons

Variations

- colored construction paper
- paste
- watercolor paints
- scissors
- ruler
- colored markers
- old magazines
- 9" x 12" (23 cm x 31 cm) drawing paper

Procedure

Practice drawing a clown holding balloons. The objects toward the back of a picture will appear smaller, and those in the foreground will appear larger. When you are finished with your drawing, color it brightly with soy crayons. To make the balloons appear three-dimensional, make the shading and any words, numbers, or symbols, on the balloons follow the curves of the balloons.

Assignment Choices

Teacher's Note: For choice #1, show students how to draw the depth of a room on the chalkboard. For choices #2 and #3, explain what a vanishing point is. Show magazine pictures of landscapes with roads or pathways disappearing in the center of the picture or take the students on a short walk and point out how the roads and sidewalks narrow and disappear in the distance.

1. On a 12" x 18" (31 cm x 46 cm) piece of white drawing paper, draw a picture of your own room or a room you would like to have. The furnishings may be construction paper cutouts, or you may draw them with markers. Add wallpaper, pictures, and other decorative touches.

2. On a 9" x 12" (23 cm x 31 cm) piece of drawing paper, draw a landscape of a road, pathway, or walk disappearing into the distance. Color the finished sketch with watercolors.

3. Look in magazines to find pictures with two vanishing points. Such a picture will have forms that are large in the middle and taper off on both sides. Then create your own picture with two vanishing points.

Connection

Charles Demuth was an artist who liked to use one, and sometimes two, vanishing points. In his painting "Figure Five in Gold," the objects are large in the foreground and become smaller in the background. Charles Demuth fools you into thinking that you are seeing deeply into the picture.

Adapting to Overlapping

Purpose of the Lesson

to show students how to create depth by placing one object over another

Art History

Stuart Davis (1894–1964) was born in Pennsylvania. He was a painter and an illustrator. His painting "Combination Concert" illustrates overlapping to create an illustration of three-dimensional depth on a two-dimensional plane.

Materials

- 9" (23 cm) paper plate
- 8" (20 cm) paper plate
- 9" x 12" (23 cm x 31 cm) tan and yellow construction paper
- markers or crayons
- pencil
- paste
- scissors

Variations

- 9" x 12" (23 cm x 31 cm) black, white, and colored construction paper
- scrap tagboard for patterns
- compass
- pictures of Mimbres pottery designs

Procedure

Trace around the edge of a 9" paper plate on a piece of tan construction paper. Trace around the edge of an 8" (20 cm) or smaller paper plate onto a piece of yellow construction paper. Cut out petals from the remaining scrap pieces. Glue the petals so they stick out from behind the yellow circle. Let the petals overlap each other. Glue the larger tan circle behind the yellow circle so that the petals are sandwiched in between. Draw a picture of yourself in the center of the yellow circle and color it with markers. Be sure to add interesting details.

Assignment Choices

Teacher's Note: For "Assignment Choice" #1, bring in pictures of Mimbres pottery designs to share with the students.

1. Study the pictures of Mimbres pottery. Draw a Native American design or a design of your choice on a piece of 9" x 12" (23 cm x 31 cm) drawing paper. Color it with a black marker or use black and white construction paper pieces. You may also wish to include black and white paper weaving as part of the design.

2. Make a pattern of a person doing something active, such as an ice skater, dancer, or baseball player. Cut out the pattern and trace it onto white construction paper. When tracing, be sure to overlap the figures (as shown in the example on the next page). Outline each figure with a bright marker, and fill it in with a crayon of the matching color. Add an appropriate background.

3. Use a piece of colored construction paper as a background. (This may be textured if you wish.) Select three colors to contrast with the background (for example, black, gray, and red). Make a simple pattern of your choice, such as a bird, apple, or airplane. Trace your pattern on each of the three contrasting colors. Cut them out, and paste them on the background in an overlapping motif. Add details with a marker.

Connection

Overlapping is a valuable technique which creates depth of field. It adds interest to a composition. The students should be encouraged to use this device often in their artwork, just as Stuart Davis did.

Slitherin' Snakes and Other Slinky Creatures

Purpose of the Lesson

to give students experience in making three-dimensional designs and to stress that three-dimensional projects have length, width, and depth

Art History

Constantin Brancusi (1876–1957) was born in Romania. He was one of the most original and influential sculptors of the 20th century. His sculpture "Bird in Space" uses metal to capture the feeling of a bird leaving the ground to soar into the air.

Materials

- construction paper
- paste or glue
- scissors
- pencil
- markers or crayons
- plastic wiggly eyes (available in craft or fabric stores)

Variations

- sturdy wire
- string or cord
- heavy cardboard
- bits of furry materials

Procedure

Make a snake or ladybug out of construction paper links.

To make the snake, cut 1" x 6" (2.54 cm x 15 cm) strips of green construction paper and make a paper chain. The one pictured on the next page has 15 links. Use the patterns on the next page to add a head and a pointed tail. Glue a forked tongue in the snake's mouth and add large,

plastic wiggly eyes. Cut and paste (or draw) small red dots and diamond shapes on the body.

To construct the ladybug, cut 3 ½" x 10" (9 cm x 25 cm) strips of orange paper and then make a short paper chain of four or five links. Cut six legs (pattern on the next page) and attach them to the top of the paper chain. Cut out a ladybug shape (pattern on the next page) and decorate it with spots. Fold the body down the center lengthwise. Tape this form to the top of the thick paper chain. Make a circular tube of paper and place it under the fold in the ladybug's back to help the creature keep its shape.

Assignment Choices

1. Make a dragon, dinosaur, frog, turtle, alligator, or other animal of your choice out of a paper chain. Choose the appropriate width of chain links to make your particular animal.

2. Use several different widths of paper chain to make an animal with legs and a tail. Add funny, large feet and a head with a humorous expression. Add wire to the legs for stability. Bits of fur, moving eyes, and a rope tail will enhance your critter.

3. Make a paper-chain wreath. A circular cardboard form will help the wreath keep its shape. Add contrasting seasonal decorations. Hang the wreath by a string.

Connection

Constantin Brancusi's sculpture "Bird in Space" is an example of art in three dimensions. It demonstrates to the students that three-dimensional art has length, width, and depth.

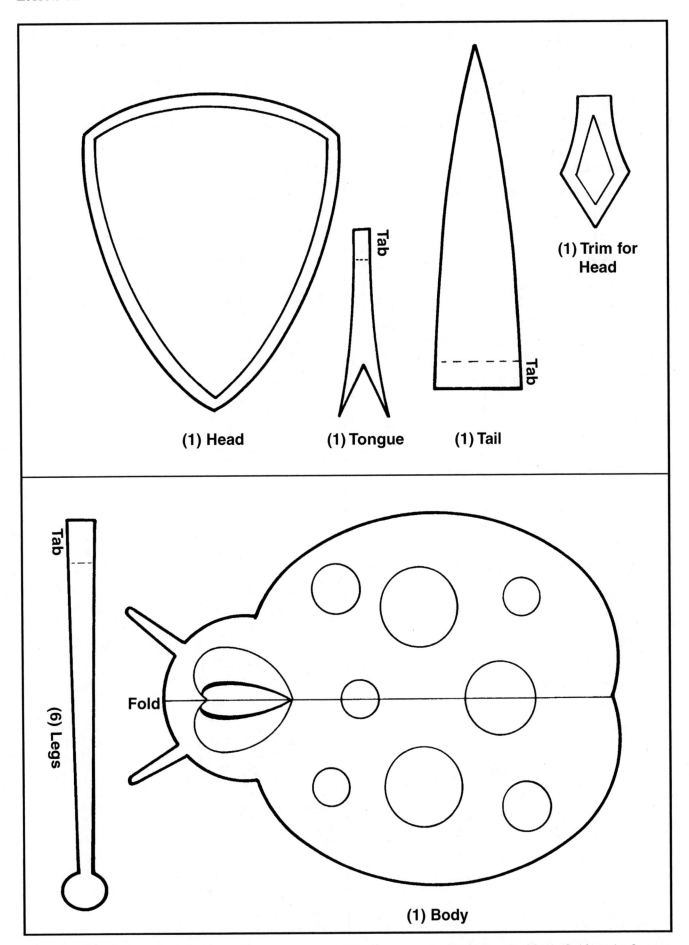

(1) Head

(1) Tongue

(1) Tail

(1) Trim for Head

Tab

Tab

Tab

Fold

(6) Legs

(1) Body

Smitten by Kittens

Purpose of the Lesson

to show the students how to establish a focal point in their compositions

Art History

Cecilia Beaux (1855–1942) was born in Pennsylvania. After her mother's early death, she was cared for by her grandmother and her aunt. Her paintings were beautifully created with complicated shading. Many consider her masterpiece to be "The Man with a Cat."

Materials

- soy crayons
- scissors
- pencil
- ruler
- gold foil
- paste or glue
- 9" x 12" (23 cm x 31 cm) white construction paper

Variations

- ¹/₂" (1.3 cm) almond-shaped, amber glass pieces (available at a craft stores)
- superhold hair spray or fixative
- paper towel
- markers
- 8 ¹/₂" x 11" (22 cm x 28 cm) black construction paper
- plastic wiggly eyes (available at craft stores)
- black ballpoint pen

Procedure

Draw a picture of a kitten and a fishbowl on 9" x 12" (23 cm x 31 cm) white drawing paper. Cut out a goldfish from gold foil and glue it in the fishbowl. Color your picture with soy crayons.

Assignment Choices

1. Draw the head of a kitten to mostly fill a 9" x 12" (23 cm x 31 cm) piece of white construction paper. Color the kitten in shades of tan and brown chalk. Give the kitten green eyes. Spray your picture with superhold hair spray or fixative. Glue amber eyes in the center of the round eyes that you drew.

2. Draw a kitten on a piece of black 8 ¹/₂" x 11" (22 cm x 31 cm) paper. Cut it out and add a pink nose and plastic wiggly eyes. Set it aside. Draw an oval rug on a piece of paper towel. Cut it out and then fringe the edges with your scissors. Decorate the rug with markers. Glue your rug to a piece of 9" x 12" (23 cm x 31 cm) white paper. Glue your black kitten to the center of the rug. Add some background to your picture, such as a window and drapes (the drapes could be made from paper towels).

3. Draw a friendly puppy and a frightened kitten. Arch the kitten's back. Use a ballpoint pen to draw its fur standing up. Color your picture with soy crayons.

Connection

In this lesson, students will learn how to add an area of interest which will act as a focal point. Cecilia Beaux's artworks can act as examples. Stressing the importance of a focal point to very young children may also be explained as a way to control the attention of the art viewer.

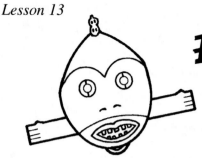

Eerie Eskimo Masks

Purpose of the Lesson

to help the students appreciate the Eskimo culture by making masks similar to those made in Greenland

Art History

Paul Klee (1879–1940) was born in Switzerland. His paintings have a child-like quality mixed with surrealism and cubism. His painting "Face of a Face" is strangely primitive and mask-like. It is similar in feeling to the Eskimo masks in this lesson.

Materials

- 9" x 12" (23 cm x 31 cm) construction paper in tan, red, dark green, yellow, orange, and black
- glue
- scissors
- pencil
- cardboard
- tongue depressors
- paper plates (optional)
- beads (optional)

Variations

- stapler and staples
- binder twine
- black marker
- brown paper bags
- brown construction paper

Procedure

To make a mask, refer to the example on the opposite page or design your own, using similar motifs. A sturdy mask can be made from cardboard or two paper plates which have been glued together. Thin paper strips work well for the teeth. Yellow beads or construction paper may be used for the eyes. Use tongue depressors for the hands. Cut the lips, chin, and hair from construction paper.

Assignment Choices

1. To make an Eskimo mask with hair, glue or staple paper from a brown bag to a sturdy cardboard or paper plate background. Cut the sides of the mask so that they are straight and round the top and bottom. To make the hair, ravel short lengths of binder twine and glue them to the top of the head for bangs. Trim the bangs if they are uneven. Glue a piece of dark-brown paper to the top of the head over the bangs. Use a marker to make a line of connected Xs (as shown). Glue on eyebrows and eyes. To form the nose, fold a nose-shaped piece of paper down the center and round the edges. Add a diamond-shaped mouth and octagon-shaped cheeks.

2. Start this mask by gluing two paper plates together for the face. Cover them with brown construction paper. Draw and cut out eyes (leave the centers open), nose, mouth, chin, and eyebrows from tan construction paper. You may wish to add colorful accents with construction paper to make your mask as individual as possible.

Connection

Paul Klee appreciated and investigated many art forms. He will inspire your students to find good things in cultures different from their own. One critic said that Klee's inventiveness was even greater than Picasso's. Students should be encouraged to also develop their own inventiveness when they make their masks.

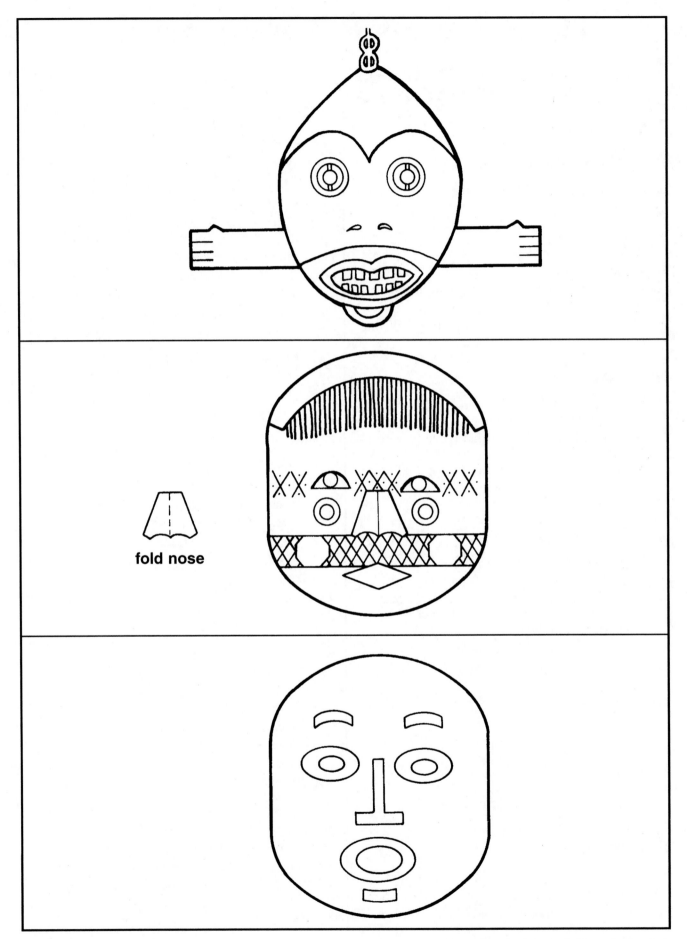

fold nose

Patriotic You with Red, White, and Blue!

Purpose of the Lesson

to help foster students' love for their country and respect for its flag

Art History

Jasper Johns (1930–) was born in Georgia. He uses many types of media in his creations, such as chalk, crayon, paint, and ink. He is also a cartoonist. His composition "Three Flags" is one of many patriotic prints he designed.

Materials

- white tagboard
- 18" (46 cm) white string
- 6" (15 cm) red plastic salad plates
- glue
- 1 yard (.91 m) of 1½" (4 cm) red, white, and blue striped ribbon
- large silver stars
- scissors
- pencil
- plastic ring

Variations

- 3" (8 cm) diameter cardboard tubes, 7" (18 cm) in length
- 1 yard (.91 m) of red or white string
- red and white construction paper
- small silver stars
- dark-blue tissue paper
- lightweight cardboard
- small brads
- markers
- soy markers
- white and blue 9" x 12" (23 cm x 31 cm) construction paper
- soy crayons

Procedure

Trace the patterns for George Washington and Abraham Lincoln (on the next page) onto white tagboard. Cut them out carefully. Glue them

onto 6" red plates. Glue the plates onto an 18" piece of red-, white-, and blue-striped ribbon. Leave about 2" (5 cm) between the plates and leave 3" (8 cm) of ribbon at the top. Attach a plastic ring to the top and staple it in place. Cut four, three-inch (8 cm) pieces of ribbon. At one end of each of these pieces, snip a *v*. Glue the ribbons to the plates as shown in diagram. Glue three pieces of string to the bottom plate and attach three silver stars (see diagram).

Assignment Choices

1. To make a patriotic windsock, cover a 7" (18 cm) tube with strips of red and white construction paper. Tie string at four evenly spaced points at the top of the tube, and tie the other end to a plastic ring. Cut ten 1" x 15" (2.54 cm x 38 cm) strips of blue tissue paper. Add small silver stars to them. Glue the blue tissue strips to the inside edge of the tube. Hang your windsock in a breezy place.

2. Celebrate our country's birthday by creating and decorating a paper birthday cake. Draw a large cake on a piece of paper and decorate it in patriotic colors and designs. Cut it out and mount it on a piece of blue construction paper. Roll up strips of construction paper to make candles (you may wish to color these to resemble firecrackers). Glue or tape the candles into place.

Connection

Jasper Johns used the simple, rectangular form of the flag to make a famous composition. This lesson will teach students that it can be an exciting challenge to take available materials to create art with a certain theme.

Awesome Animal Art

Purpose of the Lesson

to learn to draw animals in their habitats and to use imagination and design to enhance animal forms

Art History

Henri Rousseau (1844–1910) was born in France. His pictures strongly influenced surrealism. (Surrealism is a French art movement meant to give subconscious, dream-like qualities to real objects.) Rousseau was called a primitive painter because he had no formal art training. In his picture "Tiger Attacking a Buffalo" he painted each detail precisely true to life.

Materials

- colored construction paper
- chalk
- colored pencils
- markers
- acrylic paints and paintbrushes
- a long roll of paper for a mural
- pencil
- pictures of rain forest animals and plants
- superhold hair spray or fixative (to spray over chalk drawings)
- 12" x 18" (31 cm x 46 cm) white drawing paper
- plastic plate to use as a palette

Variations

- wallpaper sample books
- pinking shears
- poster board
- pictures of various kinds of animals
- pipe cleaners

Procedure

Teacher: Display pictures of rain forest animals for students to study.

When students have finished their individual animals, have them glue them to a long piece of white mural paper. Let groups of six students at a time work on painting a background for the mural. Display the completed mural in the classroom.

Student: Choose a rain forest animal and research its natural habitat. Color your animal. You may even use a combination of media (for example, markers and colored pencils). When you are finished, cut it out and glue it to the mural paper that your teacher has provided.

Assignment Choices

1. Choose a wild animal from your state, an endangered species, a farm animal, or an extinct animal. Draw your choice on a piece of paper. Research and draw its habitat. Color the picture with crayons, markers, colored pencils, chalk, and/or paints.

2. Choose an animal. Draw the animal's shape on tagboard and cut it out. Cut out squares of wallpaper with pinking shears. Paste the squares onto the animal shape to give it a calico feel. When the glue is dry, trim any excess wallpaper from around the animal shape. Add details to your animal with markers. Use other materials to add extra features.

Connection

Henri Rousseau's lack of formal artistic training did not deter him from making beautiful art. He taught himself with experimentation and practice. Through his good work habits, he became a success. Your students can also be artistically successful by using their imaginations and by practicing daily.

34

Rainforest Animal

Rainforest Animal

Endangered Animal

Endangered Animal

"Calico" Animal

"Tree-rific" Landscapes

Purpose of the Lesson

to teach students how to draw landscapes with a variety of trees, mountains, houses, buildings, roads, bushes, and flowers

Art History

Paul Cézanne (1839–1906) was born in France and became a leader in the impressionist school of painting. He chose forms from daily life, like houses, mountains, apples, and trees. He painted dense, green foliage and the light green of trees in early spring. His painting "Jas de Bouffan" shows his dynamic technique.

Materials

- 12" x 18" (31 cm x 46 cm) drawing paper
- oil crayons
- pencil
- old magazines

Variations

- pictures of rain forest trees
- gel glue or art paste
- colored pencils
- colored tissue paper
- construction paper
- brushes
- watercolor paints
- 12" x 18" (31 cm x 46 cm) white mounting paper

Procedure

Teacher: Young children tend to draw "lollipop" trees. Show them the basic structure of a tree, how the branches are attached, and the way the branches taper to a point.

Student: Study live trees outdoors or pictures of trees in magazines.

Draw various trees on a piece of paper. Add interest to the picture by including buildings, roads, bushes, flowers, and other elements. Color your picture with crayons or oil crayons. Oil crayons smear easily, so if you choose to use them, color your picture from top to bottom to avoid much of the problem.

Assignment Choices

1. Choose a tree with a distinctive shape, such as a weeping willow. Draw the tree trunk and branches on tissue paper and cut them out. Brush gel glue on the mounting paper and lay the tissue tree on top. Brush over the tissue paper with another thin layer of gel. Cut out leaves for your tree from several layers of tissue paper or construction paper. Glue them in place. Add background details with crayons. Use watercolor paints to paint the sky.

2. Make bamboo shoots by cutting strips of tan paper and drawing sections on them with a black marker or crayon. Cut out leaves from green construction paper. Glue the shoots and their leaves to a piece of sky-blue paper. Add jungle grass with a green marker.

3. Draw a tree that you could imagine might grow in a rain forest. Add leaves and vines to the tree. Create a lush landscape by adding tropical plants with flowers and large, thick leaves. Color the landscape with colored pencils or soy crayons.

Connection

Trees enhance a landscape and create a cool, peaceful mood in a composition. Paul Cézanne drew and painted trees to create breathtaking landscapes. He also used trees to create perspective, light, and shadow. The students can learn from Cézanne how to layer colors to make effective trees.

37

Purpose of the Lesson

to teach students the meaning of still-life pictures and to give examples of ways to do them

Art History

Andrew Wyeth (1917–) was born in Pennsylvania. He is known for his unique approach to the painting of genre scenes. In his painting "Wood Stove," there is a beautiful detail of a window with pots of geraniums sitting on the ledge. "Wood Stove" is a good example of a still-life picture.

Materials

- assorted colors of construction paper
- tempera paints
- paper towels
- 12" x 18" (31 cm x 46 cm) white paper
- bowl of water
- a collection of tree leaves
- paintbrushes
- a book of Native American designs
- crayons or markers
- glue
- scissors
- plastic plate for a palette
- pencils

Variations

- superhold hair spray or fixative
- chalk
- clear tape
- plastic food wrap
- research material about terrariums

Procedure

Choose a color scheme of either a light color of paper with dark or vivid paints or black paper with light colors of paint. Apply paint to the underside of a leaf (where the veins are predominant). Press the leaf on drawing paper and rub the top of the leaf to transfer the paint to the paper. Carefully pull up the leaf and repeat the process. Use several types of leaves and several colors. When your leaf prints have dried, cut them out.

Fold a piece of construction paper in half and cut out a vase shape. Decorate your vase. Arrange the cutout leaves and vase on a piece of 12" x 18" (31 cm x 46 cm) paper. Make cattails out of dark brown construction paper and add thin strips of tan paper for the stems. Glue the leaves, cattails, and vase in place.

Assignment Choices

1. Cut out thin strips of paper to make the lattice of a window. Glue them onto light-blue paper. Cut a 2" (5 cm) wide strip of paper to make a windowsill. Draw and cut out several pots and vases. Draw and cut out flowers to put in them. Glue the flowers and vases onto the windowsill.

2. Draw a terrarium. Glue on cutouts of plants, shells, stones, small logs, and other things of your choice. Cover the terrarium with plastic wrap to simulate glass.

3. Draw and cut out a fruit bowl and fruit. Using chalk color, add shadows to your bowl and fruit. Ask the teacher to spray your work with hair spray to keep it from smudging. Arrange and paste the fruit and fruit bowl on a piece of paper. Color the background.

Connection

Andrew Wyeth shows the students how to take very ordinary, everyday objects and make them into compositions of beauty and grace. The students should learn from Andrew Wyeth how to become careful craftsmen when they begin a new art lesson.

A Creative Twist to Crayon Resist

Purpose of the Lesson

to introduce students to the technique of crayon resist

Art History

Marc Chagall (1887–1985) was born in Russia. Although his family was poor, they gave him art lessons at an early age because they recognized his talent. His painting "Feathers in Bloom" depicts a fowl accented in Chagall's favorite color, blue, in close proximity to a satyr-like, blue horse.

Materials

- oil crayons
- watercolor paints
- bowl of water
- small paintbrush
- pencil
- scissors
- 9" x 12" (23 cm x 31 cm) white construction paper
- 12" x 18" (31 cm x 46 cm) white construction paper

Variations

- crayons
- 12" x 18" (31 cm x 46 cm) sky blue and pink construction paper
- blue-green paper
- paste

Procedure

Teacher: Enlarge the rooster pattern on page 41 for this activity.

Student: Choose your own subject for this activity or use the pattern on page 41. Color solidly the head, beak, and body with crayons. Trace the shape of the feathers on white construction paper. Outline the feathers with crayon, preferably a bright color. Paint over the feathers with watercolor paints. Let them dry and cut them out. Paste the feathers onto the rooster's tail. Do the large feathers first and then fill in with the smaller ones.

Assignment Choices

1. Draw an outer-space picture with planets, galaxies, stars, meteors, asteroids, etc. Carefully outline and color in (solidly) the drawing with bright colors. Paint in the background with watercolor paints.

2. Draw a large fish on white paper. If you wish, you may add smaller fish, plants which might grow in the sea, starfish, etc. Color some forms and outline others. Paint the forms you have outlined with watercolors. Cut out all of the forms and paste them on blue-green paper. Add waves and froth.

3. Divide a piece of construction paper into four equal parts. Draw forms and lines in each section. Color the lines and solid areas. Paint the background with an interesting selection of watercolors.

Connection

The students can develop many interesting textures and forms with the crayon resist technique. And, like Marc Chagall in his picture "Feathers in Bloom" they may discover a variety of subtle nuances of shade. Chagall dreamed about his childhood in Russia, and these dreams found their way into his art. His dream-like images of vibrant colors will inspire students to put some of their own experiences into their work.

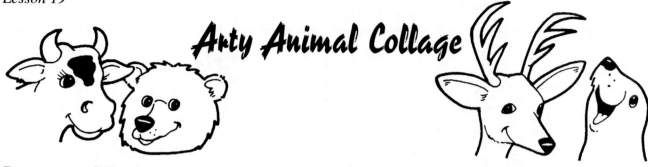

Arty Animal Collage

Purpose of the Lesson

to show students how a variety of fabrics can be used to make collages

Art History

Edward Hicks (1780–1849), a folk artist, was born in Pennsylvania. He painted over a hundred versions of "Peaceable Kingdom" His pictures show wild and tame animals living in peaceful coexistence.

Materials

- 8 ½" x 11" (22 cm x 28 cm) scrap paper
- 9" x 12" (23 cm x 31 cm) white construction paper
- scissors
- pencil
- white glue
- gray velvet fabric scraps
- heavy gray cord
- plastic wiggly eyes (available at craft and fabric stores)
- markers
- scraps of white, red, and pink construction paper
- costume jewelry beads (optional)

Variations

- brown, furry fabric
- yellow and brown printed fabric
- diamond print fabric
- various fabric scraps
- tan construction paper
- heavy yellow cord
- scraps of brown, green, and yellow construction paper

Procedure

Draw a large elephant on 8 ½" x 11" (22 cm x 28 cm) scrap paper. Cut it out to use as a pattern. Trace the pattern onto gray velvet and cut out the form. Glue (evenly) the fabric elephant onto a piece of 9" x 12" (23 cm x 31 cm) white paper. Add a tail of gray cord, frayed at the end. Attach the plastic wiggly eyes. Cut two tusks from white construction paper, a tongue from red paper, and toes from pink paper. Add a jeweled head or neck if you wish. Add details to the face with markers.

Assignment Choices

1. Draw a large monkey on 8 ½" x 11" (22 cm x 28 cm) scrap paper. Cut it out to use as a pattern. Trace the pattern onto a piece of 9" x 12" (23 cm x 31 cm) white paper. Make a face, ears, hands, and feet from tan construction paper, and glue them on. Glue on a pair of plastic wiggly eyes. Add features and details with markers. Cut out a body and tail from brown, furry fabric and glue them onto the paper. Add a red, jeweled collar from construction paper and costume jewelry.

2. Draw a large giraffe on 8 ½" x 11" (22 cm x 28 cm) scrap paper. Cut it out and trace it onto a piece of 9" x 12" (23 cm x 31 cm) construction paper. Use the pattern to cut a body from yellow- and brown- printed fabric. Glue the fabric from the neck to the knees onto the paper. Use yellow paper to make the face and the section from the knees to the feet. Make hoofs from brown paper. Add plastic wiggly eyes. Make face accents and details with markers. Add green paper leaves for the giraffe to munch on.

Connection

Edward Hicks' paintings depict themes of peace. In this lesson, students will learn to use fabric in collage and to arrange a picture to create a definite theme.

yellow and brown fabric

tiger-striped fabric

spotted, furry fabric

brown, furry fabric

diamond print

gray velvet

Woven Wonders

Purpose of the Lesson

to show students that a combination of parts can be integrated into a harmonious whole to achieve a pleasing and dynamic woven composition

Art History

Käthe Kollwitz (1867–1945) was born in East Prussia. A master draftsman, printmaker, and sculptor, Kollwitz was awarded a gold medal by the King of Saxony for a series of prints known as "The Weaver's Uprising." She used her talent in art to make social commentaries about the poor and oppressed.

Materials

- construction paper (four or more colors)
- scissors
- glue or paste
- pencil
- tape

Variations

- old magazines
- wallpaper samples
- ribbon, yarn, gift wrapping cord, etc.
- paper bag
- gift wrapping paper
- foil

Procedure

Teacher: If you are doing this activity with very young students, you might want to prepare the construction paper for them ahead of time. The border for younger students should be 1" (2.54 cm) around the construction paper. It should also be reinforced with tape underneath. Then draw six or more wavy lines, border to border, lengthwise. Cut along the lines for the students. Do not cut through the border.

Student: Choose a color of construction paper. Draw a ¹/₂" (1.27 cm) border on all sides. Then draw six or more wavy lines, border to border, lengthwise. Cut along the lines. Do not cut

through the borders.

Cut strips of varying sizes out of another piece of construction paper. Cut the strips from the width of the paper, not the length. Weave the strips in an over and under pattern on the paper that you prepared. Alternate the strip colors and widths. Paste the ends of the strips down and trim off any excess paper if necessary. Add interesting decorations of your choice.

Assignment Choices

1. Choose a color of construction paper. Draw a ¹/₂" (1.27 cm) border on all sides. Cut straight and narrow lines across the paper but do not cut through the borders. Weave strips of random widths and colors through the paper.
2. Choose a color of construction paper. Draw a ¹/₂" (1.27 cm) border on all sides. Cut zigzag lines across the paper but do not cut through the border. Cut strips of various widths from colorful magazine pictures. Weave the magazine strips through the paper.
3. Choose a color of construction paper. Draw a ¹/₂" (1.27 cm) border on all sides. Cut lines across the paper but do not cut through the border. Cut strips of wallpaper, brown paper bags, yarn, foil, or ribbon. Include some shiny strips, such as satin ribbon, gift wrapping cord, metallic thread, or fabric. Be creative!

Connection

Käthe Kollwitz showed us that art can be found in many forms. Weaving is an art form that requires much skill and patience. From this simple introduction, the students may wish to learn more about the art of weaving.

Ideas for Cutting Your "Loom"

Discover a Way to Sculpt Clay

Purpose of the Lesson

to teach students how to create three-dimensional art forms, using commercial or homemade clay

Art History

Auguste Rodin (1840–1917) was born in France. He created sculptures that showed the feelings of humanity. He sculpted the human conditions of suffering, vitality, and passion. His sculpture "Man with the Broken Nose" emphasizes the subject's inner pain.

Materials

- modeling clay
- school glue
- plastic wrap
- varnish
- newspapers
- acrylic paint
- paintbrush
- pencil, toothpick, or paper clip
- cup of water

Variations

- rolling pin
- book of Native American pottery and jewelry designs
- toothpicks
- decorative cord, elastic thread, string, or dental floss

Procedure

Create a penguin out of clay. You may choose a different animal if you wish; however, these directions are for a penguin. Roll a chunk of clay into a ball for the head. Roll a second chunk of clay into an oval for the body. Use smaller pieces of clay to make the feet, eyes, beak, and wings. Use a pencil, toothpick, or straightened paper clip to add details. Brush your sculpture with a mixture of one tablespoon (15 mL) of glue to a small cup of water. Let it dry and then paint it. When it has dried again, spray your sculpture with varnish.

Assignment Choices

1. To make Native American pottery, roll clay to flatten, or use the coil method. Make a separate, round base for either type. Incise a Native American design on the pottery. Discard any clay "crumbs." Brush on a solution of one tablespoon (15 mL) of glue to one cup of water. Dry your pottery on plastic wrap and paint it with bright colors.

2. Make round or tube-shaped beads for a bracelet or necklace. Incise holes in the beads with toothpicks. You may wish to also make a pendant, using a thin, flat piece of clay. Poke a small hole near the top of the pendant. Let the beads and pendant dry on plastic wrap and then paint them with acrylic paints. After they have dried again, string the beads and pendant on decorative cord, elastic thread, string, or dental floss.

Homemade Cornstarch Clay

Mix and blend one part cornstarch to two parts baking soda. Add one part cool water (or more, if needed). Add powdered tempera if you wish to give the clay a color. Cook and stir the mixture until it is thick but still pliable. Remove it from the heat and cover it with a double thickness of wet paper towels. Keep it covered until the mixture cools. Knead it like bread dough. After sculpting, let the sculpture air dry.

Connection

Rodin used clay to create beautiful art and then transformed his ideas into bronze sculptures. Students can also experience this three-dimensional material. They will learn to sculpt meaningful artwork just as Rodin did.

Hands-On Painting

FINGER PAINT

Purpose of the Lesson

To show students that manual dexterity is an integral part of creating art when working with certain types of media

Art History

Elaine de Kooning (1920–1989) was born in New York. A teacher at the University of New Mexico, she became interested in bullfighting and produced a series of paintings on this spectator sport. Her technique looks much like finger painting even though she used a brush to achieve the effect. "Sunday Afternoon" is the name of one of her paintings.

Materials

- 12" x 18" (31 cm x 46 cm) white paper
- finger paint
- pencil
- black ballpoint pen
- glue
- plastic wiggly eyes (from craft store)
- bowl of water
- paper towels
- newspaper
- old shirts, aprons, or smocks to protect clothing

Variations

- 9" x 12" (23 cm x 31 cm) pale yellow, sky blue, and white construction paper
- paintbrush or old toothbrush
- small cotton swabs
- watercolors and a soft watercolor brush
- toothpicks
- clothespin
- nail file
- orange stick

Procedure

Make a friendly dinosaur on a 12" x 18" (31 cm x 46 cm) piece of paper. Make a light sketch of the dinosaur with a pencil. Dampen the paper and then apply shades of green paint with your fingertips. Add grasses and plants to the background. Add teeth with a ballpoint pen. Glue on plastic eyes.

Assignment Choices

1. On a piece of dampened 9" x 12" (23 cm x 31 cm), pale yellow paper, make a landscape. Apply a circle of yellow finger paint for a sun and then brush the paint outward with a paintbrush or toothbrush. Paint trees by blotting on green paint with a crumpled piece of paper towel. Create a smooth ground with your finger. Use a cotton swab to make human figures.

2. On a piece of dampened 9" x 12" (23 cm x 31 cm) sky blue paper, make a tree. Give the bark texture by applying the paint with a wooden clothespin (the flat side). Add baby birds and a nest using your little finger. Add eyes and beaks to the birds with a black ballpoint pen.

3. Lightly sketch a pelican on a piece of 9" x 12" (23 cm x 31 cm) white paper. Dampen the paper. Water paint the upper two-thirds of paper with oranges and yellows for a sunrise. On the lower third of the paper, water-paint green for grass and foliage. Let the background dry and hen finger-paint your pelican. Paint texture on the bird; use a toothpick to make lines on the wings, a nail file to make the lines on its chest, and an orange stick to make lines on the tail.

Connection

Students can make attractive compositions by learning to paint with their fingers. They should notice that "Sunday Afternoon" could also be done with finger-painting techniques.

Fine-Tooth Comb

Crosshatch with a Comb

Pencil Eraser

Paintbrush Handle

Crumpled Paper Towel

Smooth with Finger

Wavy Lines with a Comb

Finger-prints

Exploring a Captivating Culture

Purpose of the Lesson

to introduce the students to artifacts from the Native American culture and to help them create their own artifacts from recyclable and simple materials

Art History

Rudolph Carl Gorman (1931–) was born in Arizona. His friends call him Rudy. He is one of the top 10 working artists in the United States. He is a Native American Navajo, and he began painting at the age of four. Besides being a talented artist, he enjoys good food and has written three cookbooks. His serigraph "Crystal" is a rainbow of vibrant color.

Materials

- mesh onion sacks
- binder twine
- wooden hoops, corrugated cardboard, or sturdy paper plates
- gold curling ribbon
- assorted sequins
- assorted colors of feathers
- glue
- scissors

Variations

- tagboard
- masking tape
- crayons or markers
- #20 brown grocery bags
- pencil
- stapler and staples
- construction paper (optional)

Procedure

Native American (Ojibway) mothers hang dream catchers above their children's beds. It is said that these trap bad dreams while letting the good dreams pass through.

You can make your own dream catcher, using a 9" (23 cm) wooden hoop, a ring of thick cardboard or a ring cut from a sturdy paper plate. Cut out a circle of onion bag mesh and glue it to the back of the ring. Wrap binder twine around circle and glue it firmly in place. Glue a few sequins to the front of the mesh. Add feathers and curling ribbon as shown on the following page. Allow two ribbons to hang down about 12" (31 cm) and attach feathers to them. Hang the dream catcher over a bed.

Assignment Choices

1. ***Arm Band:*** Cut a 15" x 1¼" (38 cm x 3 cm) band from tagboard. Paste a 3" (8 cm) circle in the center of the band. Paste two layers of feathers around the center circle. Decorate a 1½" (4 cm) circle and paste it over the feathers so that the feathers are sandwiched between the two circles. Decorate the band. Fasten the ends together with staples or masking tape. Wear on your upper arm.

2. ***Vest:*** Cut the bases off two grocery bags. Split down one side of each bag so that they lie flat. Iron the pieces if needed. Cut out two front pieces and one large back piece as shown on the following page. Decorate the vest pieces with Native American designs. Staple or glue your vest together along the side and shoulder seams. For extra strength, line the vest with brightly colored construction paper. Add paper fringe if you wish.

Connection

As students imitate the art of the Native Americans, their knowledge and appreciation of a culture very different from their own will grow.

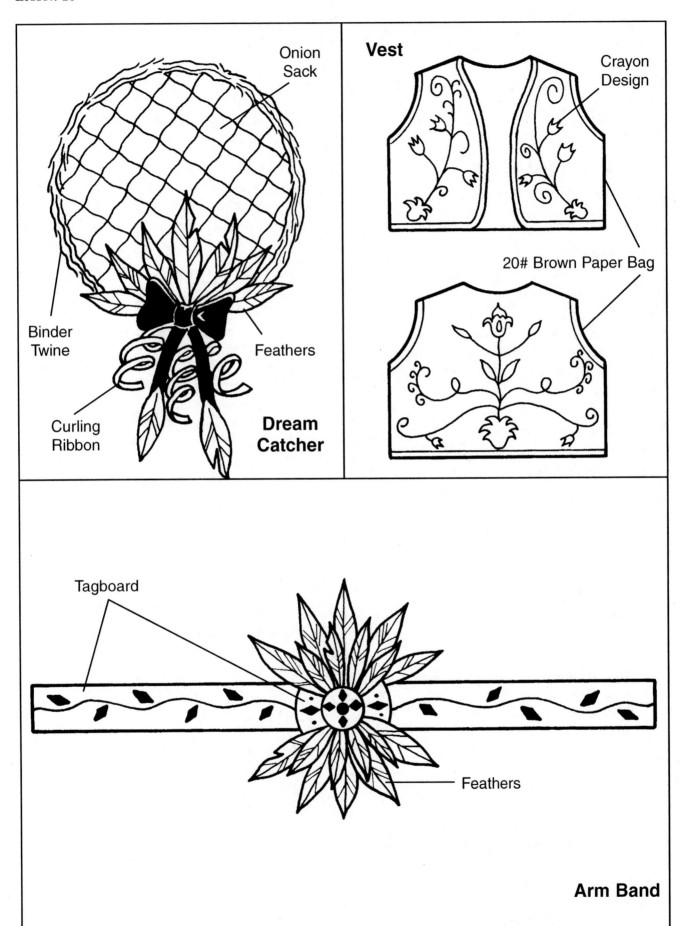

Onion Sack

Binder Twine

Curling Ribbon

Feathers

Dream Catcher

Vest

Crayon Design

20# Brown Paper Bag

Tagboard

Feathers

Arm Band

Plunge in with a Sponge

Purpose of the Lesson

to introduce the students to the technique of sponge painting to achieve value and texture

Art History

Claude Monet (1840–1926) was born in France. He was a leader and member of the impressionist group of French painters. Monet used a technique of side-by-side colors that allows the eye to blend them at a distance. His painting "Chrysanthemums" is a good example of this technique.

Materials

- various colors of tempera paint
- sponges (synthetic)
- 12" x 18" (31 cm x 46 cm) white drawing paper
- pencils
- markers
- paint palette
- water
- brush for mixing
- reference books

Variations

- colored construction paper and scraps
- paste
- colored pencils
- small paintbrush

Procedure

Study some pictures of sunflowers. Sketch a picture of sunflowers in a vase. Mix tempera paint to a medium consistency. Use white to lighten a color and black to make darker shades of a color. Dip a small piece of sponge into paint and apply it to a piece of scrap paper to test out the consistency of the paint and to get used to the sponge-painting technique.

Apply paint to your sketch. Sponge-paint the background around the sunflowers. Create light and dark areas to add interest to the composition. When your picture is dry, outline it and add details with a black marker.

Assignment Choices

1. Select a colorful and exotic bird such as the quetzal, scarlet ibis, great bird of paradise, cock-of-the-rock, blue honeycreeper, village weaverbird, Lady Amherst pheasant, emerald cuckoo, or macaw.

   Sketch the bird and its habitat. Use a sponge or brush to paint the background in tempera paint. Then sponge paint over the bird sketch.

2. Draw an interesting bowl, plate, or compote and cut it out of construction paper. The dish should be rather large. Draw a variety of fruit on construction paper scraps which will fit in your dish. Before cutting out the fruit, sponge on deeper shades of the same color as the construction paper to make the fruit look three-dimensional. Cut out the fruit and paste it in the dish, overlapping it to make an interesting composition. Mount the dish and fruit on paper of your choice and add accents with a brush.

Connection

Claude Monet created his chrysanthemums by using splashes of light and dark colors. The students can learn from Monet how to create effective texture and value.

What Lives in a Pond?

Purpose of the Lesson

to give the students experience in constructing dioramas and to present a simple concept of pond life

Art History

Camille Pissarro (1830–1903) was born on Saint Thomas Virgin Islands in the Caribbean. He became the founder and leader of the impressionism movement. He was outstanding in encouraging children to develop their artistic talents. His painting "The Pond at Sunset, Montfoucault" shows the play of light on the pond surface in early evening.

Materials

- 9" or 12" (23 cm or 31 cm) sturdy paper plates
- colored and white construction paper
- light-blue paint and paintbrush
- small, flat pebbles
- small rocks
- plastic wiggly eyes
- fine-tip markers
- paste
- tape
- plastic wrap
- scissors
- black ballpoint pen

Procedure

Create a pond by pasting two plates together (for strength). Paint the inside of the pond light blue with wavy lines to simulate water. Let the paint dry. Wash and dry small pebbles. Glue them onto the plate.

Choose some plants and animals to decorate in and around your pond. When you are finished arranging and securing the plants and animals, stretch plastic wrap over the top of the plate. Secure the plastic wrap on the back with tape.

Fish: Cut out five fish shapes (see the next page). Decorate both sides of the fish with fins, scales, and eyes. Cut slits in the plate. Pull the fish tabs through the slots and tape them underneath.

Turtle: Cut out two identical turtle shapes (see the next page). Decorate one turtle and leave one plain. Roll a small strip of paper and glue it to the middle of the plain turtle. Lay the decorated turtle on top and glue the pieces together to give the turtle thickness. Glue the turtle in the pond.

Water Lilies: Cut out flowers from white paper and water-lily leaves from green paper. Bend the petals of the flowers up along the dotted line. Glue the flowers on top of the leaves. Not every leaf needs a flower. Attach these to the pond after it has been covered with plastic wrap.

Snake: Cut out a green snake, using the pattern on the following page. Decorate the snake with markers and fold it as shown. Paste a red tongue to the mouth. Add plastic eyes.

Frog: Paint a small rock green to make a frog. Let it dry. Add dark-green spots. Pick a side for the face and glue on plastic eyes. Add a small, diamond-shaped, red mouth. Glue it to the edge of the pond.

Ducks: Cut out several ducks (see the next page) on the fold of a piece of white paper. Fold and glue the tabs on each duck together. Glue the ducks on top of the plastic wrap.

Connection

Camille Pissarro showed the effect of light on a pond. In this lesson, the students will show a pond as a habitat supporting life.

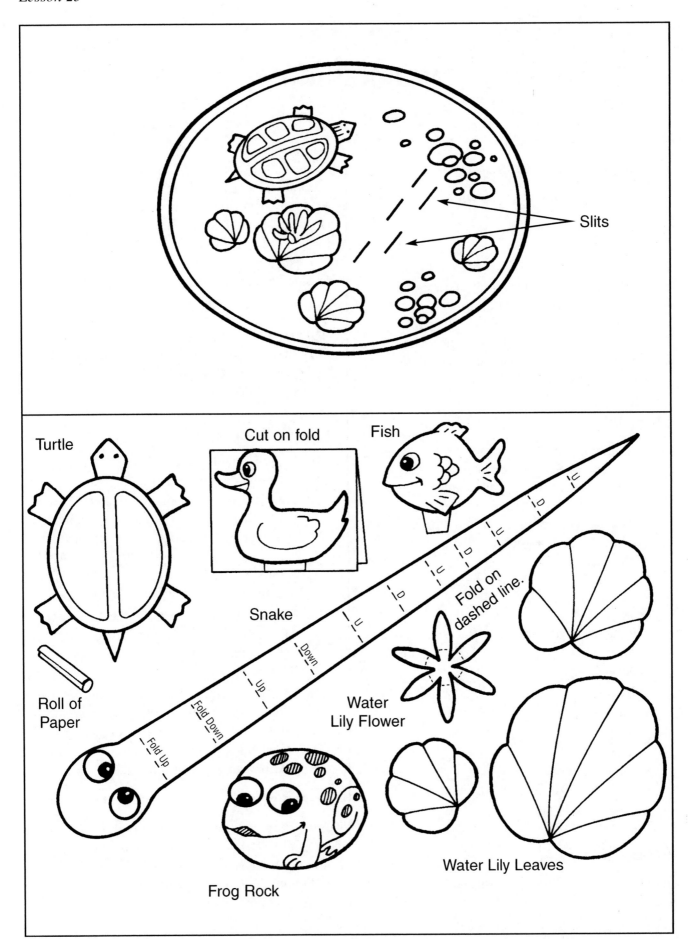

Slits

Turtle

Cut on fold

Fish

Snake

Fold on dashed line.

U
D
U
D
U
Down
U
Fold Down
Up
Fold Up

Roll of Paper

Water Lily Flower

Frog Rock

Water Lily Leaves

Stencil and Sponge Pictures

Purpose of the Lesson

to teach students the art of stenciling

Art History

Paul Signac (1863–1935) was born in France. He worked with Georges Seurat to develop the technique of pointillism. Pointillism uses a collection of dots which blend together when viewed from a distance. His painting "The Pink Cloud" gives the viewer an ethereal feeling of unusual delicacy and refinement.

Materials

- small sponges
- 6" (15 cm) Styrofoam plates
- tempera paint in red, yellow, green, and brown
- 9" x 12" (23 cm x 31 cm) tan, brown, and white construction paper
- glue
- pencil
- leaves
- crayons
- light cardboard or plastic
- cups
- paper towels

Variations

- paper doilies
- string
- scissors
- colored pencils
- 12" x 18" (31 cm x 46 cm) white construction paper
- markers or pen

Procedure

Teacher: Put the paints on disposable plates on a table covered with protective plastic. Provide sponges, water cups, and paper towels.

Student: Make a pattern for a bushel or decorative basket on scrap paper. Cut it out. Trace the pattern on a piece of 9" x 12" (23 cm x 31 cm) tan construction paper. Cut lines in the basket and weave dark brown strips of paper through the lines. Add small amounts of glue to keep the strips in place.

Make an apple-shaped stencil. On white paper, sponge-paint six separate apples and then let them dry. Cut them out and mount them and the basket on construction paper. Add paper or real leaves as accents.

Assignment Choices

1. Draw a butterfly on 12" x 18" (31 cm x 46 cm) construction paper. Cut it out. Use the paper that the butterfly was cut from as a stencil. Place the stencil on another piece of paper and sponge-paint in bright colors to make a butterfly. Add details with a marker. Lace a string through the center of it and hang it.

2. Make a drawing of a fall scene. Make and use a pumpkin stencil for your picture. Color stalks of corn with a colored pencil. Sponge-paint a blue sky.

3. Paint a snowman. Cut circles out of a paper doily to make stencils. Use white tempera paint, a sponge, and your stencils to paint the head and body of your snowman. Add details with a pen or marker.

Connection

In Paul Signac's painting "The Pink Cloud" the color of each dot contrasts with the one next to it, but at a distance, they blend. The students will blend their colors by using a sponge, simulating pointillism.

Mosaic Medley

Purpose of the Lesson

to teach the art of making mosaics, using a variety of inexpensive and readily available materials

Art History

Fernand Léger (1881–1955) was born in France. He used manufactured objects as a springboard for creating new work. He developed a style using colorful light and dark geometric shapes, as can be seen in "Leisure: Homage to Louis David."

Materials

- various colored sequins
- bristol board or tagboard
- glue
- pencil
- scissors
- hot glue gun (for the teacher)
- small safety pins

Variations

- newspaper
- 9" x 12" (23 cm x 31 cm) black construction paper
- aluminum foil
- black cardboard
- construction paper scraps
- small cereal boxes
- assorted pasta (such as vermicelli and wide noodles that can be broken)
- hole puncher
- string
- markers

Procedure

Teacher: Use a hot-glue gun to attach a safety pin to the back of each student's finished artwork.

Student: Make an artistic badge which represents yourself. Draw a circle 3 ½" (9 cm) in diameter on lightweight cardboard. Draw a design on the circle that is a symbol of yourself. Glue sequins to outline your design. Then fill in your design with sequins of the same and/or contrasting colors. After your teacher has glued on a safety pin, wear your badge proudly.

Assignment Choices

1. Draw buildings on scrap paper. Cut out the buildings and trace them on newspaper and black construction paper or lightweight black cardboard. Cut the newspaper buildings into mosaic pieces. Paste the newsprint pieces onto the black buildings. Leave some of the black showing between the mosaic pieces. Use aluminum foil for the windows, stars, and moon.

2. Draw a creative picture of the sun on a piece of black cardboard (see the next page). Fill in the sun with assorted pasta. Glue the pasta in place and let it dry. Color the pasta with brightly colored markers.

3. Cover an individually-sized cereal box with construction paper. Sketch (in pencil) a design of your choice on the front and back of the box. Use a hole puncher to punch dots from scrap construction paper. Fill in your design with the dots and glue them in place. Punch holes at the top of the box, and insert a string for hanging.

Connection

Fernand Léger was inspired to create new art pieces from the ordinary things around him. The assignments may also cultivate a sense of inspiration as students imitate Leger's placement of complementary color combinations.

Wild Weather

Purpose of the Lesson

to help students understand that the disciplines of art and science can be combined to make meaningful compositions

Art History

George Inness (1825–1894) was born in the state of New York. He was known as the father of America's landscape painting. One of his paintings, "The Coming Storm" gives the viewer a feeling of impending severe weather.

Materials

- 9" x 12" (23 cm x 31 cm) light blue construction paper
- colored chalk
- superhold hair spray
- pencil
- white or iridescent glitter
- paste
- markers

Variations

- 9" x 12" (23 cm x 31 cm) blue-green, gray, yellow, purple, and black construction paper
- scissors
- pencil
- foil
- white puff paint

Procedure

Teacher: Before this activity, you may want to share with your students "The Great Wave" by Japanese artist Hokusai.

After the activity, spray the students' artwork with superhold hair spray or fixative.

Student: On light blue construction paper, make a pencil sketch of a stormy sea with big waves. Draw a boat in the water and scenery along the shoreline. Color it with chalk. Add white or iridescent glitter to the waves to look like foam. Add details to the picture with markers.

Assignment Choices

1. Make a late evening scene showing an electrical storm on blue-green construction paper. Cut out thin lines from the scene in the shape of lightning bolts and paste foil behind the cutouts. Add houses, trees, buildings, a water tower, etc. Add angry clouds in purple, black, deep blue, and green and a hazy, pale moon.

2. Create a picture of a tornado, vertically, on a piece of gray construction paper. On the horizon line near the bottom of the paper, make a rolling landscape from purple and yellow pieces of paper. Draw a narrow funnel cloud that starts on the horizon and reaches to the top of page. Add swirling clouds around it. Draw a roofless house on the horizon line. Draw objects from the house in the swirling clouds. Color your picture with markers.

3. Draw a lake with some bare winter trees. Color the lake with a blue crayon. Puff-paint snow on the ground and clouds in the sky. Draw colorful skaters and a snowman. Apply thin lines of glue in swirling patterns to simulate a blizzard. Glue on white or iridescent glitter.

Connection

Challenge the students to imitate George Inness' ability to make the viewer sense the weather being portrayed. Other paintings depicting weather that might also inspire the students are "Stormy Waters" by Anna Cohran, "October" by Willard Metcalf, "Sunset" by Winslow Homer, "Floating Ice" by Claude Monet, and "Winter Scene" by Pieter Breugel.

61

It's a Wrap!

Purpose of the Lesson

to teach the students a printing process while exploring a variety of paper textures

Art History

Lee Krasner (1908–1984) was born in New York. She married the famous artist Jackson Pollock. Krasner's art is abstract expressionism with surrealistic tendencies. Her painting "Abstract No. 2" shows a persistent repetition of forms with constant variations.

Materials

- newspaper
- white wrapping paper or tissue paper
- potatoes or turnips
- tempera paint
- sturdy disposable plate
- paring knife for the teacher
- orange stick
- scissors
- pencil
- spoon
- paper towels
- pen or thin marker
- paintbrush

Variations

- white paper bags
- purple or yellow shelf paper
- colored markers

Procedure

Teacher: Before beginning this activity, cut the potatoes in half.

Student: Sketch a simple design on the flat side of a potato half and then use the tip of a spoon or some blunt scissors to carve out the design. Use an orange stick to clean up the design. Pour a small amount of paint on a disposable plate and spread it evenly on the plate with a paintbrush. Dip the potato into the paint and check to make sure that the paint is evenly covering the potato design. Print your design onto white butcher or tissue paper. Butcher paper may be easier to use. Let the paint dry and use the paper as gift wrap.

Assignment Choices

1. Make a design for birthday wrapping paper. Cut a design into a potato half; for example, a candle, cake, present, or number may be used. Dip the potato design in paint and print it. You may wash off the paint in between prints and then use other colors. Writing "Happy Birthday" between the prints will enhance the gift wrap.

2. Celebrate Valentine's Day by making card holders out of white paper bags (lunch-sized). Carve a heart into a half potato. Make red and pink heart prints on your paper bag. To further decorate your bag, integrate your name or initials into the design. Place your Valentine cards in the bag.

3. On purple or yellow shelf paper, design an Easter motif. Eggs, bunnies, Easter baskets, or lilies, may be used. Dip the potato design in paint and print it. You may wash off the paint in between prints, and then use other colors. Print on the shelf paper and accent it with markers.

Connection

Learning to carve basic forms and learning to use a simple printing process are very important. From Lee Krasner, the students can learn about the dynamic placement of forms and good color combinations.

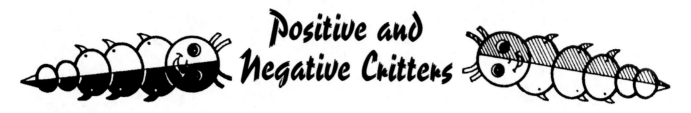

Positive and Negative Critters

Purpose of the Lesson

to guide the students in the use of contrast in art and to give them an overview of symmetry

Art History

Edouard Baldus (1813–1889) was born in France. He established early standards for fine photography. His photograph "Pont du Gard, Nimes" is clearly defined in black and white and is reminiscent of the positive/negative technique.

Materials

For All Creatures:

- scraps of red construction paper
- plastic wiggly eyes (available at craft stores)
- assorted yarn, old beads, glitter, etc.
- paste
- scissors
- pencil
- markers
- ruler
- black ballpoint pen
- two colors of scrap paper

Bug: dark- and light-green construction paper

Kangaroo: gray and yellow or light- and dark-gray construction paper

Cat: brown and orange construction paper

Bunny: tan and pink or gray and pink construction paper.

Procedure

Teacher: Use the patterns on the opposite page but enlarge them to fit 8 ½" x 11" (22 cm x 28 cm) paper, or the students may design their own symmetrical patterns.

Student: Lay the center line of the bug on the edge of light-green construction paper. Cut out

the half pattern, and lay it aside. Repeat the same steps with the dark green paper. Paste the light half to a dark green background and the dark half to a light green background. Align the two halves so that they make a whole bug and carefully paste a backing to the pieces.

Add plastic wiggly eyes and red spots cut from construction paper. Use markers to add other details and decorations.

Assignment Choices

Choose the cat, kangaroo, or rabbit pattern, or make your own symmetrical pattern of an animal of your choice. (If you should choose to make your own pattern, outline only half of the animal and use it twice so that the sides are exactly symmetrical. Test your pattern on a piece of scrap paper first to make sure it looks attractive when it is doubled.) Trace a half-pattern on two contrasting colors of paper. Cut out the two halves. Paste the halves on backgrounds of the opposite colors. Align the two halves so that they make a whole animal and carefully paste a backing to the pieces. Use markers to add details and decorations. If you choose to make a kangaroo, add a pouch. If you make a cat, add a tail to one side. Add whiskers and/or a yarn bow tie to a rabbit. Be creative when you add the details to your animal.

(**Note:** An interesting alternative to using solidly colored backgrounds would be to use plain paper for one side and printed paper, such as gift wrap, for the other.)

Connection

Edouard Baldus used contrast in his compositions to make them dynamic. Bright contrasts will enhance the positive/negative designs of the students.

Monoprint Monsters

Purpose of the Lesson

to introduce students to another type of printing process, the monoprint

Art History

Henri de Toulouse-Lautrec (1864–1901) was born in France. Leg injuries in his childhood caused him to be disabled. He was a fine artist, creating many oil paintings and prints. His lithograph "Ambassadeurs" is one of his famous poster prints.

Materials

- 12" x 18" (31 cm x 46 cm) nonporous surface such as glass, Plexiglas, or plastic
- brayer
- water-based printing ink
- drawing paper
- butcher paper
- tagboard
- paper towels
- tools for drawing: orange stick, toothpick, pencil, small brush, bristle brush, etc.

Variations

- scissors
- paste
- colored paper
- a collection of leaves and grasses

Procedure

Place ½ teaspoon (2.5 mL) of water-based printing ink on the glass or plastic surface. Roll it out with a brayer. (If you do not have a brayer, roll three or four paper plates in a tight roll and smooth the ink with the smoothest side.) Add enough ink to cover the size of the picture you are going the create.

Using a pencil eraser, small brush handle, or orange stick, draw a picture of a sea monster in the ink. Add texture with a narrow bristle brush or other tool. Press a piece of paper carefully over the drawing. Smooth it with your hands so that the paper will accept the print. Pull the paper off carefully and let it dry. Frame your print with a tagboard frame or mount your picture on a tagboard rectangle.

Assignment Choices

1. Use the same directions as in the "Procedure" section to draw a more human type of monster who lives in a cave. Add horns and teeth. Make your print on pale-green or gray paper.
2. Gather small leaves, grasses, and other foliage. Apply a thin coat of printing ink with a brush. Print several types of foliage on white drawing or butcher paper. Be sure the veins of the leaves make a good print. Let them dry. Use the printing ink to create a picture of a bird-like monster. Make a print on white drawing paper and let it dry. Cut out the bird monster and foliage but leave about ⅛" (.3 cm) of white paper around the forms. Arrange them on sky-blue or yellow paper and paste them down securely.
3. Create a scary picture of your choice in the printing ink. Print your picture and let it dry. Print leaves on several colors of paper and let them dry. Cut out all of the prints. Choose another color of paper (neutrals are good) and paste the forms on it to make a nice composition.

Connection

Using printing ink and making prints requires practice in order to make prints with good lines and contrast. Henri de Toulouse-Lautrec spent much time perfecting his technique. If students' prints do not turn out as expected, remind them that it sometimes takes time and patience to achieve a desired effect.

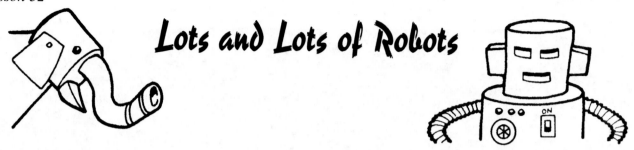

Lots and Lots of Robots

Purpose of the Lesson

to challenge the students to use their imaginations to create attractive art pieces from material scraps

Art History

Alice Aycock (1946–) was born in Pennsylvania. An innovative artist, she works with heating coils, sheet metal, motors, fans, and rubber tubing. She constructs huge, non-functional, machine-like sculptures such as "The Savage Sparkler."

Materials

- metallic spray paint (gold, silver, or bronze)
- glue
- scissors
- hot-glue gun, if needed (See note below.)
- 1/8" or 1/4" (.3 cm or .6 cm) thick plywood
- research materials

Other Suggested Materials

small boxes, straws, toothpicks, plastic lids and caps, small plastic containers, buttons, string, plastic tubing, dowels, wooden drawer pulls, plastic bolts and gears, washers, marbles, hinges, cardboard, paper clips, etc.

A Note About Materials: Primary-age students should only work with paper, wood, and plastic when constructing their robots. This way they can use regular glue to put their creations together. If metal pieces are used, arrange for adult volunteers to use hot-glue guns to assemble the robots. *The students should never use hot glue guns.* Even for adults, have cold water available in the event of a hot-glue accident.

If you use metal materials, here are some suggestions: gears, bolts, nails, springs, pieces of old alarm clocks, bearings, washers, and wires.

Procedure

Construct a homework robot. Use your imagination and gather materials to make your own version of a homework robot. Decide how you would like to arrange your materials and then glue them together. Ask your teacher to spray your robot with metallic paint. Attach your robot to a square plywood base. Write some simple directions for using your homework robot.

Assignment Choices

1. Design a house-cleaning robot to help out in your family's home. You may draw it or make a three-dimensional model out of items you have gathered.
2. Choose an animal. Make a model robot of the animal out of items you have gathered. Mount your animal on a plywood base. Write a short piece about what your robot animal can do that is different from the real animal.
3. Research dinosaurs. Choose a favorite dinosaur and construct a replica of it from the items you have gathered. If you need a certain shape and do not have it in your collection, you may cut pieces out of cardboard. Glue the pieces together and ask your teacher to spray your artwork with metallic spray. Mount your dinosaur on a plywood base.

Connection

Just like Alice Aycock, students should construct their projects in a spirit of fun. Her artistic machines are only made to be decorative. None of them actually work, but she enjoys the challenge of breaking up space in innovative ways.

Tackling Turkey Day

Purpose of the Lesson

to teach the students to create artwork that celebrates a holiday theme while integrating history, art, and culture

Art History

Nathaniel Currier (1813–1888) was born in Massachusetts. James M. Ives (1824–1895) was born in New York. These artists formed a lithograph publishing firm which published a variety of genre scenes of late 19th century history, such as "Home for Thanksgiving."

Note to the Teacher: Grandma Moses' painting "Home for Thanksgiving" may also offer inspiration for these projects.

Materials

- string or yarn
- ziti pasta
- small hole punch
- markers
- pencil
- scissors
- construction paper of various colors

Variations

- paper plates
- curling ribbon
- tagboard
- nuts (hickory, acorn, etc.)
- small pine cones
- ruler
- marker
- glue
- 12" x 18" (31 cm x 46 cm) white paper
- crayons or colored pencils
- hot-glue gun (for the teacher)

Procedure

Make a fruit necklace. Use the patterns on the next page or design your own to make the fruit. Cut out the fruit and then punch a small hole near the top of each piece. Lace the fruit on yarn or string, alternating with ziti pasta (as shown in the diagram). Add details to your fruit with a marker. Write things that you are especially thankful for on the back of the fruit.

Assignment Choices

1. Glue two paper plates together for strength. Cut out the centers of the plates. Trace around real leaves (or sketch your own) on fall-colored construction paper. Cut out enough leaves to cover the paper-plate wreath. Glue the leaves in place. Ask an adult to hot-glue nuts and a bow on your wreath. Hang it by attaching a loop of string on the back.

2. Make a bracelet out of a ¾" (2 cm) wide strip of tagboard. Decorate it with construction paper turkeys and pumpkins; use the patterns on the next page or design your own. Add details with a marker. Staple or glue the ends of the bracelet together.

3. Read the story (or have an adult read the story) of the first Thanksgiving. On a piece of 9" x 12" (23 cm x 31 cm) white paper, draw a picture of how you envision the first Thanksgiving Day. Use crayons or colored pencils.

Connection

Students may wish to make a picture of Thanksgiving as we know it today. In all these projects, students should use the same care and concern for detail that Currier and Ives showed in their genre pictures.

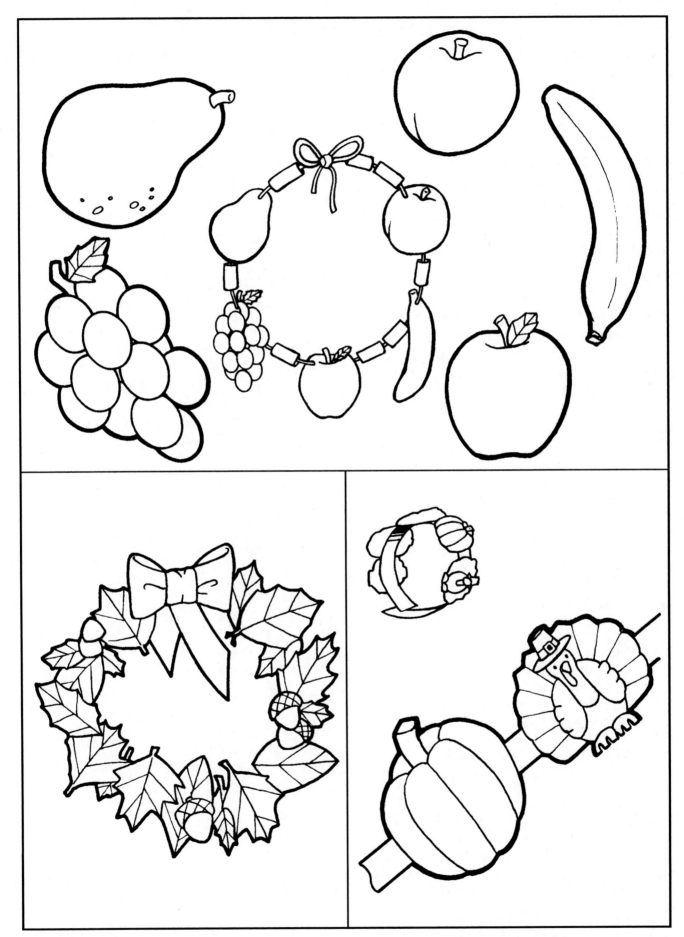

71

Crafty Christmas Creations

Purpose of the Lesson

to make decorative Christmas tree trimmings from simple materials

Art History

Grandma Moses (Anna Mary Robertson, 1860–1961) was born in the state of New York. Her painting, "Out for Christmas Trees" is one of her best-known paintings. Perhaps it is so popular because of its decorative touches and details. Grandma Moses was a true American primitive, as was her style.

Materials

- white tagboard
- silver glitter glue
- paste
- scissors
- pencil
- clear tape
- green, plastic clothespins

Variations

- assorted colors of velour paper
- black construction paper
- dried corn kernels or dried peas
- gold spray paint
- small pot of dirt
- slender green dowel

Procedure

Trace and cut out two bird bodies, two wings, and one tail from white tagboard. (See the next page for patterns.) Paste the bird body pieces together but do not paste the bottom tabs together. Cut two slits in the body of the bird, one at the tail and one on the side, as shown. Insert the tailpiece into the appropriate slot and secure it with a piece of tape. Insert a wing on

each side and paste each securely. Bend the tabs outward along the base of the bird. Glue the tabs to the top of a clothespin. Accent the tail and wings with silver glitter glue and clip your bird to the branch of a Christmas tree.

Assignment Choices

1. From scrap paper, make a pattern for a Christmas tree. Cut the tree from tagboard to use as a base. Cut out layers of branches from different colors of velour paper. Overlap them on the tree base and paste them in place. (See the next page.) Paste a star on top. Mount your tree on black construction paper. Accent it with silver glitter glue.

2. Make a holiday flower. Cut the center circle of the flower from a piece of tagboard. Paste dried corn kernels or dried peas in the center of the circle. Spray the circle with gold paint. Cut out six large and six small petals from red velour paper. Paste them around the outer ring of the circle in a large-small-large-small pattern. Attach the flower to a slender green dowel. Add green velour leaves and place it in a small pot of dirt.

Connection

Grandma Moses used simple materials to make her paintings. Similarly, the students can use simple materials and careful craftsmanship to make attractive Christmas decorations.

tail-cut 1

wings-cut 2

slash
all lines

bird body-cut 2

flower center

flower petals
cut 6 of each

leaf-cut 4 or
more

Have a Heart!

Purpose of the Lesson

to give students the experience of using shapes and overlapping to create holiday projects and pictures

Art History

Howardena Pindell (1943–) was born in Pennsylvania. She works with many materials and techniques, such as collage, paint, various materials for sculpture, and video drawings. Her composition "Temple: Part of India" is mixed media.

Materials

- colored construction paper
- glue
- scissors
- pencil
- crayons

Variations

- hole punch
- various colors of tissue paper
- tempera paint
- paintbrush
- water
- tagboard or plastic lid
- string
- sponges
- brown paper bags
- parchment paper or used dryer sheets
- white and/or brown paper bags

Procedure

Trace and cut out the peacock pattern pieces on the next page. Color the bird's eyes and beak with crayons. Begin by gluing the head-pieces together but do not glue the base of the necks. Fold outwardly along the dotted lines at the base of the necks. Fold the body and wing hearts in half and

glue them together as shown. Glue the head and tail to the body as shown. Cut out smaller hearts to use as decorations. Attach thin legs made of stiff paper.

Note: The patterns may be enlarged if you wish.

Assignment Choices

1. Place two pieces of red paper on top of each other. Cut out a large heart shape so that you have two identical hearts. Cut out the centers of the hearts about $\frac{1}{2}$" (1.3 cm) from the edge. You should then have two heart frames. Paste a piece of parchment paper or a used dryer sheet to one of the frames. Trim away excess paper from the outside edges of the heart. Glue irregularly-sized pieces of tissue paper (various colors) to the parchment paper. Glue the other heart frame over the parchment paper (so that it becomes sandwiched between the two frames) to give it strength. After it has dried, punch a hole at the top and attach a string for hanging.

2. Draw and cut out stencils for hearts, heart-shaped leaves, and stems. These may be cut from lightweight cardboard or from thin, plastic lids. Cut out a flower pot from construction paper and glue it to drawing paper. Stencil flowers, stems, and leaves coming out of the pot, using small sponges dipped in tempera paints.

Connection

In Howardena Pindell's "Temple: Part of India," she used many shapes, colors, patterns, and textures to create a distinctive work. Students should imitate her ability to explore a variety of media to create their heart projects.

74

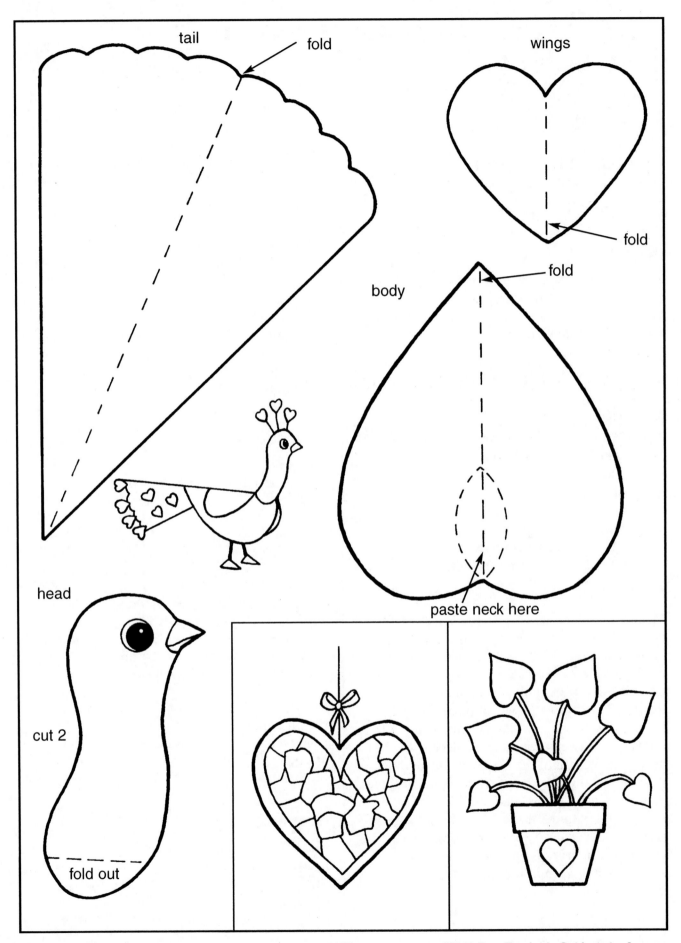

tail

fold

wings

fold

fold

body

paste neck here

head

cut 2

fold out

Presents for Parents

Purpose of the Lesson

to teach the students how to create handmade gifts to honor their parents

Art History

Mary Cassatt (1844–1926) was born in Pennsylvania. In her painting, "The Boating Party," she introduces us to a young family, out for a ride in a sailboat.

Mother's Day

Materials

- clear, clean plastic lids (such as the ones from deli pint containers)
- glue
- scissors
- pencil
- flower seed catalog
- colored construction paper scraps
- glitter glue or baking crystals

Procedure

Make a set of coasters for Mother's Day. Use two lids of the same size per coaster. Cut brightly colored flower pictures out of a seed catalog (see approximate size on the next page). Choose scrap-paper colors to blend with the flowers. (See the example on the next page.) Paste a flower on one color and cut $1/8$" (.3 cm) around the flower. Repeat these steps with different colors until the flower and its outlines fit snugly within the rim of a lid. Trim away the outer, raised lip of a second lid. Fit this circle over the lid with the flower. Fill (from the back side) the indented section of the coaster with glitter glue or crystals and glue. Make four coasters with different flowers and color combinations.

Father's Day

Materials

- 9" x 12" (23 cm x 31 cm) white paper
- rubber bands
- cardboard tube
- straight pins
- corrugated cardboard
- ruler
- wood-grain contact paper
- scissors
- pencil
- brown curling ribbon
- markers
- clear tape
- hot-glue gun (for the teacher)
- white glue

Procedure

Make a memo pad for your dad's desk. Cut two $3^1/4$" (8 cm) diameter circles from corrugated cardboard. Cover the circles with contact paper; trim off the excess. Punch a hole in the center of each circle. Cover a $3^1/4$" (8 cm) long cardboard tube with contact paper also. Have an adult hot-glue the circles to the tube to make a spool. Cut nine 3" x 12" (8 cm x 31 cm) strips of white paper and paste them, end to end, to make one long strip. (**Note:** If you wish, perforate 3" [8 cm] sections of the strip with a pin. This will make it easier for your dad to rip off a piece of paper.) Paste or tape one end of the paper strip to the tube. Roll the strip onto the tube. Secure the paper on the roll with a rubber band. Insert a ribbon through the tube and the holes in the centers of the circles. Tie the string for a handle. Decorate the sides of the spool as you wish. Store a ballpoint pen in the spool, as shown.

Connection

Mary Cassatt created a dynamic and heartwarming picture from a blank canvas. Students should learn from Mary Cassatt that creative and useful gifts may be made from everyday materials, imagination, and effort.

Art Lesson—Generic Form

Purpose of the Lesson

Art History

Materials

Art Lesson—Generic Form *(cont.)*

Procedure

Assignment Choices

Connection

Art Sources

───────────────────────── **Books** ─────────────────────────

Barnes, Rachel, et al. *The Twentieth Century Art Book.* (The Phaidon Press, Ltd., 1996) *(Lesson 26)*

Fleming, William. *Arts and Ideas.* (Holt, Rinehart and Winston, 1986) *(Lesson 29)*

Heller, Nancy. *Women Artists: An Illustrated History.* (Abbeville Press, 1991) *(Lessons 2, 22, 32, 36)*

Hoving, Thomas. *Two Worlds of Andrew Wyeth: A Conversation with Andrew Wyeth.* (Houghton Mifflin Company, 1978) *(Lesson 17)*

Janson, H. W. with Dora Jane Janson. *History of Art.* (Harry N. Abrams, Inc., 1965) *(Lesson 21)*

Jeffrey, Ian. *The Photo Book.* (text only) (The Phaidon Press, 1977) *(Lesson 30)*

Kallir, Otto. *Grandma Moses.* (Harry N. Abrams, Inc., 1975) *(Lessons 33, 34, 35)*

Kelder, Diane and J. Carter Brown. *Great Masters of French Impressionism.* (Crown Publishers, Inc., 1980) *(Lesson 37)*

Klein, Mina C. and H. Arthur Klein. *Life in Art.* (Holt, Rinehart and Winston, 1972) *(Lesson 20)*

Shikes, Ralph and Paula Harper. *Pissarro: His Life and Work.* (Horizon Press, 1980) *(Lesson 25)*

The Shorewood Collection. (Shorewood Fine Art Reproductions, Inc., 1994) *(Lessons 1, 4, 5, 7, 8, 9, 10, 11, 12, 13, 14, 15, 16, 19, 24, 27, 28, 31, 34)*

───────────────────────── **Web Sites** ─────────────────────────

Romare Bearden's "The Morning of the Rooster" *(Lesson 3)*
  • http://upenn.edu/ARG/archive/Bearden.html

R. C. Gorman's "Crystal" *(Lesson 23)*
  • http://www.highfiber.com/~/1hb crystal.htm

Getty Education Institute for the Arts (Provides a variety of helpful elementary lesson plans.)
  • http://www.artsednet.getty.edu/

Prang Crayon Web site (Provides *Prang Fun Pro Soybean Crayon Product Fact Sheet* and other information.)
  • http://www.dixonticonderoga.com/dixonpr.html